DEACON MANUAL
CARING

VOLUME II

Deacon Manual
Volume II: Caring

© 2012 Brethren Press

Published by Brethren Press®, 1451 Dundee Avenue, Elgin, IL 60120.
Visit www.brethrenpress.com for publishing information.

All rights reserved. The publisher of this book hereby grants permission to any congregation affiliated with the Church of the Brethren to reproduce worship resources, provided that no part of such reproduction is sold or distributed beyond services held in the local church and provided that proper credit is given both to the original author (if noted) and to the *Deacon Manual*.

Unless otherwise noted, scripture quotations are from the New Revised Standard Version of the Bible, © 1989 National Council of the Churches of Christ in the United States of America. Used by permission. All rights reserved.

Library of Congress Control Number: 2012940895

ISBN: 978-0-87178-181-9

16 15 14 13 12   1 2 3 4 5

Printed in the United States of America

TABLE OF CONTENTS

Preface v

1. **How to Use this Volume**
   The Power of Prayer 2
   Scriptures in Ministry. 7
   Hymns as Ministry. 11
   The Ordinances 12

2. **Crises of Mind, Body, and Spirit**
   Addiction 14
   Domestic Violence and Abuse 22
   Illness, Injury, Surgery 28
   Natural Disaster 37
   Reconciliation 41

3. **Transitions**
   Children Leaving Home. 47
   End of Life 53
   Loss. 62
   Relocation and House Blessings. 67
   Separation and Divorce 74
   Caregiving 81

4. **Celebrations and Milestones**
   Birthday 85
   Anniversary 89

    Arrival of a New Child 92
    Meal Blessings 96

5. Church of the Brethren Ordinances
    The Ministry of Anointing 100
    Love Feast and Communion 128
    Believers Baptism 148

Full List of Scriptures 151
Index 179

PREFACE

Now during those days, when the disciples were increasing in number, the Hellenists complained against the Hebrews because their widows were being neglected in the daily distribution of food. And the twelve called together the whole community of the disciples and said, "It is not right that we should neglect the word of God in order to wait on tables. Therefore, friends, select from among yourselves seven men of good standing, full of the Spirit and of wisdom, whom we may appoint to this task, while we, for our part, will devote ourselves to prayer and to serving the word."

—*Acts 6:1-4*

While the title is not specifically used, this passage from Acts 6 is generally considered to describe the calling of the first deacons: people of outstanding character willing to be guided by the Spirit, with the practical ability to solve problems.

Deacon ministry in the Church of the Brethren is grounded in these same principles today. Working closely with pastors and the congregation, deacons are caregivers who are called to discern the ever-changing needs of the faith community and to serve to meet those needs.

Discernment. Service. Caregiving. These are not simple tasks, and over the years deacons have asked for help in knowing how to best fulfill their calling. That help has been provided in large part through the original edition of the *Deacon Manual for Caring Ministries*, that familiar burgundy book with thoughts on everything from deacon and pastor relationships to recipes for communion bread. It has served as the textbook for innumerable deacon meetings, and has offered up scriptures, prayers, and other aids for worship and pastoral care. This revision offers new examples of how the work of deacons is being carried out, a revised structure (and index) to make finding information easier, and expanded prayers and other pastoral care resources reflecting the changing needs of our faith communities.

With a focus on the *calling* of deacons, Volume I is designed as a reference book. What are deacons in the Church of the Brethren called to do, in broad terms? Most deacons spend a great deal of time visiting with others—in homes, in hospitals, in nursing care. How can that time be best spent? How might new deacons be selected and nurtured, and what might their relationships with the pastor and the congregation look like? Spiritual vitality in this ministry is critical, yet many question whether they are "good enough" to be deacons. In short, where do deacons go for more help on how to best serve the faith community? This is the volume to use at home, during deacon meetings, and as you reflect on your ministry during times of prayer and meditation. In other words, this is the volume that helps deacons understand and prepare for their ministry.

Volume II is the *caring* component, the book to carry along as deacons offer pastoral care and provide other types of interpersonal ministry. This volume contains a comprehensive set of prayers for many situations, as well as suggested hymns, scriptures, and other helps to be used during time spent with others. Many deacons also assist with the ordinances in their congregations, so options for preparation and services are also included in Volume II.

As you begin to use these volumes, you will see that its creation is the result of the contributions of many people. Special thanks goes to the denominational deacon ministry group itself, which has changed in name and participants between the time this project was initiated and the time of publication. These dedicated deacons, past and current, include Amy Beery, Scott Duffy, Steve Fritter, Bernie Fuska, Steve and Linda Hollinger, Lester and Barbara Kesselring, Carol Kurl, Donna McAvoy, Dale and Beverly Minnich, Mary June Sheets, and Wayne and Evelyn Zook. Several persons also contributed to these volumes based on their specific expertise, including Joshua Brockway, Kim Ebersole, Leslie Frye, Sonja Griffith, Bob Gross, Rachel Gross, Joel Kline, and John Wenger, all of whom have shared excellent words of insight and encouragement. Many thanks also go to James Deaton, managing editor of Brethren

Press, as well as Wendy McFadden, publisher of Brethren Press, Jonathan Shively, executive director of Congregational Life Ministries, and Jeff Lennard, Brethren Press marketing and sales director, whose advice was invaluable during the revision process.

Finally, I want to thank the authors of the many original prayers, as well as the contributors of the recommended scriptures and hymns. Special thanks goes to David Doudt, who coordinated the efforts of many of these contributors. The work included in these volumes is truly thoughtful, God-inspired, and much appreciated.

This edition of the *Deacon Manual* will likely—hopefully—not be the last. Our world is changing, our congregations are changing, our denomination is changing, the church universal is changing. How will the role of deacons change as our churches evolve, as our world continues to evolve? Throughout this manual is a call to continually reevaluate the needs of the faith community, and modify the service you offer accordingly. A corollary to that call, or perhaps a different way to look at it, is the invitation to continually reconsider the *possibilities* that exist in deacon ministry. How might you transform your deacon ministry to truly continue the work of Jesus?

Donna Kline, director
Deacon Ministry
Church of the Brethren

1
How to Use this Volume

Deacon ministry is one of the ways we become the hands and feet of Jesus, as the church is called to do. As such, in many ways deacons represent and bring the caring and support of the faith community with them as they offer their ministry in homes, hospitals, nursing facilities, or anywhere else an opportunity to share the love of Christ exists.

Sharing the love and encouragement of the church family can be challenging. How do we take the sense of community felt in the church along with us in our ministry? Much of what we hold dear as we worship together are the comforting words of hymns and scriptures, the peace of personal and corporate prayers. Sharing these encouraging components of worship outside of the sanctuary or fellowship hall can be a bit intimidating to lay ministers like deacons: What scriptures fit this situation? How do I pick an appropriate hymn? What will I say when I pray?

This volume has been designed to help answer these questions. Subtitled "Caring," this book is the one you will carry with you as you offer pastoral care and provide other types of interpersonal ministry. It contains a helpful collection of prayers for many situations, as well as hymns, scriptures, and other helps to be used during time spent with others.

Each of the next three chapters focuses on a broad category of life situations: (1) crises of mind, body, and spirit; (2) transitions; and (3) celebrations and milestones. Within each chapter several subcategories exist, and within each subcategory are found a number of very specific prayers, scriptures, and hymns, each with its intended audience in mind.

Even with the specificity of these resources, you may find that something listed in one section is quite appropriate for a different situation, with minor modification. As such, you are encouraged to read through all of the prayers, making handwritten notes and cross-references to help you in your ministry. Space has been provided in this manual for just that.

The Power of Prayer

> Rejoice in hope, be patient in suffering, persevere in prayer.
>
> —*Romans 12:12*
>
> Likewise the Spirit helps us in our weakness; for we do not know how to pray as we ought, but that very Spirit intercedes with sighs too deep for words.
>
> —*Romans 8:26*

How to Use this Volume 3

There is something awesome and mysterious about the very act of prayer. If God knows better than we what we need or desire, why should God be informed by us? However, it is God who calls us to prayer, God who desires our participation in the conversation.

Prayer is praise. Prayer is petition for us and for others. Prayer is a plea for protection. Prayer is how we ask for forgiveness. Prayer is our living conversation with God.

The community of prayer is a powerful gift to God's people. In the Scriptures we see the people of Israel praying to God—in homes, in the wilderness, in the tabernacle, in the temple. In the stories of Daniel, the four friends—Daniel, Shadrach, Meshach, and Abednego—gather to form a community of prayer when they are facing oppression and waiting for God's guidance. Jesus prayed regularly—alone and with people—and he taught his disciples how to pray. His followers gathered in the upper room after the crucifixion, and again after the resurrection, to pray. The Holy Spirit was first given to the gathered community at Pentecost, as the people prayed and worshiped. And in Paul's letters, there is constant exhortation to prayer.

Brethren believe in the priesthood of all believers. All believers may approach God in confidence. Any person may speak or pray for all. The one who prays may pray alone, or may lead others in unison prayers or litanies. These may be spontaneous prayers, original compositions, or prayers taken from worship manuals. The most important thing to remember is that prayer is not performance. It is part of a living dialogue.

Prayer is available to all people, a way of being with God—speaking, asking, listening, waiting, and growing. There is no requirement for prayer to be performed in a particular way, apart from the guidance of the Lord's Prayer. Nevertheless, throughout the Scriptures and the church's life, we see how God's people are strengthened when they pray together.

A Basic Framework for Prayer

The Lord's Prayer, in addition to being an ideal prayer, provides a framework for other prayers. It begins with an address to God ("Our Father in heaven") and praise of God ("Hallowed be your name") that has nothing to do with what we want God to do for us. An expression of the desire for God's will to be done ("Your will be done, on earth as it is in heaven") places our own petition in proper perspective. Then the petition ("Give us this day our daily bread") follows, an encouragement to ask for specifics—and not simply spiritual things. A request for forgiveness, coupled with a resolution to take action ourselves ("Forgive us our debts, as we also have forgiven our debtors"), is followed by a spiritual request ("Do not bring us to the time of trial, but rescue us from the evil one"). Most people close the Lord's Prayer with the doxology: "For the kingdom and the power and the glory are yours forever."

Following the pattern given in the Lord's Prayer, here is a basic framework for prayer:
- Address to God
- Statement of praise
- Affirmation of God's will
- Our petitions
- Request for forgiveness
- Resolve to do or be
- Spiritual requests
- Praise of God

When deacons are visiting someone who has lost a loved one, this prayer framework might be utilized in this manner:

"Dear God, in the midst of our sorrow we praise you. We pray that your will might be done, even in our sorrow. We come to you asking for courage and comfort for this family in their grief. In this difficult time we depend upon your strength, not our own. Forgive us our sins as we strive to do your will. Bless all of us, for we need you in our lives. Though a loved one has passed away, O God, you are a living presence in our lives, and we praise you for that. We pray in your Son's name. Amen."

It is important to be honest in prayer, especially in crisis situations. To pretend that somehow a tragic event is not tragic is to lie to God. To pretend we are pleased with events that have shattered our lives is to lie to God. Prayer is our honest conversation with One who cares.

Praying the Psalms

There is great strength in praying the Psalms, which have been the property of God's people for thousands of years. The Psalms, when prayed with and for others, bring us into communion with people around the world. We become one with believers in the past who have prayed these words, and we are one with believers of the future who will pray these same words. We pray for those things closest to our heart, and we are lifted beyond ourselves to pray for that which matters to many others. Praying the Psalms creates a wonderful sense of belonging and Christian community, and often brings needed comfort and peace.

Helps for Leading Prayer

The best form of advanced preparation for prayer is to take advantage of the many prayers written by others—available online, on bulletin covers, in worship resources, and in the pages that follow. Most of these prayers are ready to use and can be tailored to fit a particular circumstance. Praying written prayers does not mean these prayers are impersonal. In fact, they often reflect much care and devotion, as the prayer is first prayed during preparation, and then again during the prayer time with others.

There are times when deacons may be asked to pray without prior notice, such as prayers before meals. These prayers need not be long. If a framework or pattern is developed and followed, the addition of a single sentence or two regarding the particular circumstance (birthday, anniversary, wedding, funeral, etc.) will allow almost any table grace to serve. The same is true when deacons are asked to pray during times of crisis; the event may require a particular prayer, but the framework of the prayer need not change.

Scriptures in Ministry

> All scripture is inspired by God and is useful for teaching, for reproof, for correction, and for training in righteousness, so that everyone who belongs to God may be proficient, equipped for every good work.
> —*2 Timothy 3:16-17*

The Bible is more than a book; it is a library. The very name, Bible, might be translated as "The Books." Within its pages are guidelines, edification, comfort, challenge, wisdom, encouragement, and salvation.

The Bible is God's book for God's people. Though Brethren may not agree in all particulars about their understanding of certain texts, they do agree that the New Testament is their creed, the "rule of faith and practice" (1998 Annual Conference statement).

The Scriptures as a Deacon Resource

The Bible is a great resource for the deacon body. Within its pages is life itself. In addition, verses and passages provide the words deacons often need in various situations.

There are many translations of the Bible now available—the King James Version, the *New International Version*, the *Contemporary English Version*, the *Common English Bible*, and *The New Revised Standard Version* are just a few. And for some occasions reading from a paraphrase, such as *The Message* or the *New Living Translation*, is appropriate and gives fresh perspective. Deacons will want to be familiar with different expressions of God's Word, and choose the translation that speaks most appropriately and clearly to each audience and in each situation.

Note: The scripture texts provided at the end of this volume, which are referenced at the end of Chapters 2 through 4, come from *The New Revised Standard Version* unless noted otherwise.

Effective Scripture Reading

Reading scripture requires a sensitivity to its intent. Most of the Old and New Testaments was written in the vernacular—the common and ordinary language of the people of that day. It was not a special elevated language of "thees" and "thous." Indeed, the Greek of the New Testament is business Greek, the kind used as a second language by most people in the Roman Empire at the time of the writings. This language corresponds to the English used throughout the world today, a language that expresses ideas in a universal way.

The very act of reading scripture is also an act of interpretation, because the reader brings his or her experience and understanding to the reading. Scripture should be read with a deep and profound respect, but a false dignity or reverence stands in the way of understanding. Those who lived and spoke through God's Word did not always use a slow, stilted, and overpronounced cadence. They laughed and cried. They were frightened, amazed, overjoyed, inspired, depressed, angered, and relieved. They reasoned with their listeners; they cajoled, pleaded, berated, and rejoiced with their fellow believers.

When deacons are called upon to read scripture, it is always good to read and study the passage ahead of time if you are able. This becomes a time of Bible study for the reader. Is a particular passage poetry? Then the reading will require recognition of the cadences of Hebrew poetry. Is it one of the parables of Jesus? The tone of a storyteller might be appropriate. Is it wisdom literature? A matter-of-fact tone of common sense might be in order. If these are the words of one of the prophets, then a more commanding tone would be helpful. If there is more than one speaker in the passage, then more than one reader or a different tone of voice might be appropriate.

Modern English should usually be the preferred choice when reading scripture for others to hear. However, there are occasions, such as funerals or memorial services, when scriptures such as Psalm 23 should be heard in the familiar and powerful cadences of the King James Version. And for some occasions and audiences, a more recent translation or a simply worded paraphrase might speak God's Word most clearly.

Deacons will want to be sensitive to both the occasion and the audience so they do not unknowingly exclude people by their language choices. For example, some congregations welcome the sharing of scripture in a contemporary language version, in words they might speak themselves. Others hear the Word of God more clearly in a traditional translation. Just as the apostle Paul counseled some believers to avoid eating meat offered to idols if it would offend other believers, so we must not provide unnecessary language roadblocks to our brothers and sisters.

Another aspect of language of which we should be aware is the native language of members of the congregation. If you are a minority in your faith community, you know that it can be very meaningful to hear or read a prayer, sing a hymn, or share scripture in your native language. This is also an excellent reminder to the rest of the congregation that we are all children of God.

The best approach when practicing and reading scripture is to focus on the natural meaning of the text and to read in a clear and natural voice. And don't let the pronunciation of certain words prevent you from reading with confidence. Relax; your sisters and brothers in the faith are listening to you, and they are not judging you by your ability to read in public. They are hungry for God's Word and are glad that you are feeding them.

Hymns as Ministry

> Let the word of Christ dwell in you richly; teach and admonish one another in all wisdom; and with gratitude in your hearts sing psalms, hymns, and spiritual songs to God.
>
> —*Colossians 3:16*

Many of the ministries of deacons include the opportunity to use hymns, whether praying the words of favorite hymns or singing them with others. Many such occasions arise: the service of anointing, love feast, visitation in homes or hospitals, at various times of crisis, at fellowship dinners, and other times when God's people gather.

Although some deacons may feel that they have little talent for singing or leading music, most people can lead a stanza or two of a favorite hymn when the occasion arises. Often it is enough for the leader to begin the first line of a familiar hymn; others will join in and sustain the song. Remember that these occasions are not times for musical purity, they are times to raise our voices in praise of God or to pray the words of the lyrics. Many prayer and music resources are found in *Hymnal: A Worship Book* and the *Hymnal Supplement*, and hymn suggestions for use in specific circumstances are a component of each of the chapters that follow in this volume. Note, too, that the hymnal itself includes a topical index with entries including courage, doubt, forgiveness, reconciliation, and many others.

The Ordinances

> The fear of the LORD is pure, enduring forever; the ordinances of the LORD are true and righteous altogether.
> —Psalm 19:9

Deacons are often responsible for assisting with or occasionally administering the ordinances of anointing, love feast, and communion. Participating in baptism services is also something with which deacons might be asked to help. The final chapter in this volume offers background in the historical role of deacons with these ordinances, as well as thoughts on how to prepare for and carry out these roles today.

2
CRISES OF MIND, BODY, AND SPIRIT

By definition a crisis is a turning point, a time in one's life when and where an event occurs that will change the course of life forever. Often a crisis is imposed and unexpected—natural disasters such as fire and flood, a sudden illness or injury. A person or a family can be the victim of physical or sexual assault, a robbery, or some other crime. Bad choices and inappropriate behaviors reach the point of addictions. All of these involve the loss or the threatened loss of security, sameness, and a way of life. These times and happenings are frightening; they are also times of action for the deacon body. They are times for reconciliation.

Deacons are called to be holistic caregivers, striving to meet the physical, emotional, and spiritual needs of those in the congregations they serve. Crises affect each of these areas, and we are called to provide support for all. Thoughts on offering physical help are described in Volume I of the *Deacon Manual*, in the chapters on advocacy and support, health and healing, unity and reconciliation, and the ministry of visitation and presence. The prayers, scriptures, and hymns that follow are provided as helps during the times you are present with those in the midst of a crisis, offering support for healing of the mind and spirit.

ADDICTION

Prayer for the person with an addiction

O God, we lift up *(name)* to you, who you know is struggling. Help *(name)* understand that *(he/she)* is powerless against this thing, God. But we believe you when you say that nothing in all creation can separate us from your strength and your love. We believe that you are the Power above all powers. Bring *(name)* to the place of trust and belief in your power over this addiction. When *(name)* calls on you during the day or in the night, hear and answer. Give strength when there is no strength. Give hope when hope is small. We count on your promise to never give up on us. Amen.

—*Linda Alley*

Prayer for the person with an addiction

God of all compassion, you know our weaknesses and you see our hidden shame, yet you promise that you will never leave us nor forsake us. We pray now for your Spirit to be at work in the life of *(name)*, that you would break the hold of addiction and ease *(his/her)* suffering. Restore *(him/her)* to health and wholeness. May *(he/she)* sense an outpouring of your mercy and love. We ask these things in the powerful name of Jesus, the Christ. Amen.

—*Karen Allred McKeever*

Prayer for the person with an addiction

Loving God, we kneel before you now with *(name)* by our side. We come before you asking for guidance and strength, with gratitude for a chance to change things. This addiction is bigger than any of us, and *(name)* asks for your backbone and your power to see *(him/her)* through this time. God, as *(name)* seeks treatment, therapy, or whatever will help *(him/her)* through these trials, help *(him/her)* to see your work in *(his/her)* life. Help *(name)* to feel your hand at *(his/her)* back and your love in *(his/her)* heart. We ask for trust, patience, and a continual sense of hope in these trying times. Please give *(name)* the courage to ask for help and the humility to accept it, as well as the pride to remember how far *(he/she)* has already come. In your name, Lord, we pray. Amen.

—*Cassidy McFadden*

Prayer for the person with an addiction

Dear God!
Your people are vessels, open to healing light!
But we are overwhelmed by disease.
We use drugs.
We spew anger into our relationships.
Forgive us.
We covet clean air, yet we smoke.
We relish slim bodies, yet we overeat.
We decry stress, yet we overwork.
Forgive us.
We are people who neglect our physical needs.
We are people not motivated to simple living.
We are people who persist in unsatisfactory relationships.
Forgive us.
God, with your healing light, your people will be healthy.
Your people will be holy temples.
Your people will be overflowing vessels of wholeness. Amen.

—*Tana Durnbaugh*

Prayer for the person with an addiction, following a relapse

Loving God, we lift up our *(sister/brother)* *(name)* to you today. Help *(him/her)* see that a few steps backward is not a reason to

give up, that it does not mean failure. Bathe *(him/her)* with your merciful, loving, shepherding presence. Give *(him/her)* courage and strength to tackle the addiction again and break the chains holding *(him/her)* back from living a full life in you. In the name of God, the healer of all ills, we pray. Amen.
—*Nan Erbaugh*

Prayer for friends and family

Healing God, we come to you in support of __(name)__, praying for your healing power. This family has all been affected in some way by the addiction that has become such a big part of __(name's)__ life, and we ask for healing for all of us. Please help __(name)__ find *(his/her)* way back to your loving, healing presence. We know the grace you give us can work miracles; we ask that you provide the miracle of healing. Amen.
—*Terrilynn Griffith*

Prayer for friends and family

Compassionate God, give us the strength to support __(name)__ as *(he/she)* does the difficult work that lies ahead of *(him/her)* as we travel this road to healing and reconciliation together. We know there are no quick fixes; please be with each of us, every step of the way. Amen.
—*Terrilynn Griffith*

Prayer for friends and family

Loving God, we know that ___(name)___ is hurting in ways that only you can see. Help us as *(his/her)* friends and family, as followers of Christ, to offer compassion, love, and support; keep us from judgment, harsh words, or unreasonable expectations. Amen.

—Terrilynn Griffith

Prayer for friends and family

God, help us to love each other as you love us. Remind us that no one is perfect, and that we can do more in this world by love than by any other means. Just as there is room in your love for everyone, so let there be room in our hearts. Amen.

—Joy Struble

Prayer for all

Lord, it is not your will that the least of your servants should stumble. Nevertheless we know that all have sinned and fallen short of the glory of God. Now we ask that where there is brokenness, there might be healing; where there is despair, there might be hope. Help us to be the instruments of your peace. Help us to be the church for people who are hurting. Help those who are hurting to remember that you are with them.

We know that life is filled with little deaths and little resurrections. It is so hard

Resolving Disputes in Business Matters

As recorded at 1 Corinthians 6:1-8, the apostle Paul discussed lawsuits between fellow believers. He expressed dismay that some Christians in Corinth would "dare to go to court before unrighteous men." (Verse 1) Paul gave strong reasons why Christians should not sue one another in secular courts but rather settle disputes within the congregation setting. Let us consider some of the reasons for this inspired counsel and then touch on a few situations not necessarily covered by this directive.

If we have a business dispute with a fellow believer, we would first of all seek to handle matters Jehovah's way, not our own. (Proverbs 14:12) As Jesus showed, it is best to settle a disagreement quickly before it escalates into a major issue. (Matthew 5:23-26) Sadly, though, some Christians become overly contentious, even taking disputes into secular courts. Paul said: "It means altogether a defeat for you that you are having lawsuits with one another." Why? A key reason is that such proceedings may well reflect poorly on the good name of the congregation and the God we worship. We therefore take to heart Paul's question: "Why do you not rather let yourselves be wronged?" —Verse 7.

Paul also reasoned that God has given the congregation a fine arrangement for settling many disputes. The elders are Christian men made wise by their knowledge of Scriptural truths, and Paul says that they are "able to judge between . . . brothers" when it comes to "matters of this life." (Verses 3-5) Jesus showed that disputes involving serious wrongs, such as slander and fraud, should be settled according to a three-step process: first, endeavoring to settle the matter privately between those involved; second, if the initial step fails, bringing along a witness or two;

Christian elders should give careful consideration to an accusation that a Christian refuses to support his family. Refusal to care for one's family may result in disfellowshipping.

Extreme physical abuse. An abusive spouse may act so violently that the abused mate's health and even life are in danger. If the abusive spouse is a Christian, congregation elders should investigate the charges. Fits of anger and a practice of violent behavior are grounds for disfellowshipping.—Galatians 5:19-21.

Absolute endangerment of spiritual life. A spouse may constantly try to make it impossible for the mate to pursue true worship or may even try to force that mate to break God's commands in some way. In such a case, the threatened mate would have to decide whether the only way to "obey God as ruler rather than men" is to obtain a legal separation.—Acts 5:29.

In all cases involving such extreme situations as those just discussed, no one should put pressure on the innocent mate either to separate or to stay with the other. While spiritually mature friends and elders may offer support and Bible-based counsel, they cannot know all the details of what goes on between a husband and a wife. Only Jehovah can see that. Of course, a Christian wife would not be honoring God or the marriage arrangement if she exaggerated the seriousness of her domestic problems just to live separately from her husband, or vice versa. Jehovah is aware of any scheming behind a separation, no matter how one may try to hide it. Indeed, "all things are naked and openly exposed to the eyes of him with whom we have an accounting." (Hebrews 4:13) But if an extremely dangerous situation persists, no one should criticize a Christian who, as a last resort, chooses to separate. In the final analysis, "we shall all stand before the judgment seat of God."—Romans 14:10-12.

Notes:

DOMESTIC VIOLENCE AND ABUSE

Prayer for the victim

How unfair it is, God! Homes are supposed to be places where we go to be safe, but here there is hurt and fear. Give _(name)_ wisdom beyond *(his/her)* own, wisdom to try to understand the person once trusted, but who now can change so quickly into someone else, and wisdom to know how to keep *(himself/herself)* and _(the children or others)_ safe. But most of all, God, help _(name)_ to find a safe home and security in you. Amen.

—*Linda Alley*

Prayer for the victim

We cry out to you against this horrific wrong that _(name)_ has endured. Remind us that when you look at _(name)_ you do not see a victim, but one of your own children whom you love. We know you grieve with us, God. Show _(name)_ that you are the kind of parent who intends only good things for your children. Help *(him/her)* to find a safe place in your love, a healing place in your presence, a place of refuge for all the days of restoration ahead. Return trust and joy to _(name's)_ life and give *(him/her)* hope for a better future, we pray. Amen.

—*Linda Alley*

Prayer for the victim

Precious Lord, in the midst of so much stress, we are thankful that you are a God of love. I pray that somehow *(name)* , too, can believe that, in this midst of this unimaginable situation. I pray that you can sense God's presence walking with you through these days. Even though it may not feel this way now, God is ever present just as the sun is always present, even on cloudy days. You are not alone. I pray a blessing of peace for you, a deep peace that can give you strength to face these times. In the spirit of Jesus who showed God's love throughout his life, we pray. Amen.

—*Dorotha Frye-Mason*

Prayer for the victim

O God, the one who sustains us and protects us, we ask for your presence now to be with our *(brother/sister)* *(name)* . *(He/She)* has experienced a violation not caused or invited by *(him/her)*. God, provide the strength for the next part of the journey. Allow us, God, to be part of the yoke to ease the burden. Amen.

—*Blaine Miner*

Prayer for the victim

God of Peace, we come before you this day seeking your healing presence.

We come carrying the scars of physical and
  emotional abuse.
We come as people who have been hurt and
  as people who have hurt others.
Let us know and feel your peace.
Heal us where we are wounded, and use us
  as instruments of wholeness in the lives of
  others.
In the name of Christ, we pray. Amen.
—*Robert Blake*

Litany of compassion for victims of abuse
The God of Love has invited all who labor
  and are heavy-burdened to seek support
  and strength.
We come with our burdens and feel that
  we are not always in control of our lives.
Our God who acts as a loving parent welcomes us,
  promising to share our burdens.
But some of our abuses and hurts are so deep
  that we don't expect healing.
Our Creator made us to be loved and to be
  lovers.
Love is powerful!
  But hurt and pain are powerful, too.
Jesus said, "Blessed are those who mourn
  for they will be comforted."
Help us to feel welcomed, loved, and comforted
  in this community of faith.

—*Chuck Boyer*

Prayer for the abuser

Merciful God, we lift up *(name)* , who is now someone we don't understand, someone walking a path we would not choose. Lord, be with our *(brother/sister)* during this ordeal. Place your people in *(his/her)* way to lead the lost back to you. Amen.

—*Blaine Miner*

Scriptures

Psalm 22:1-2 *(for victim)*
Psalm 25:1-10 *(for victim)*
Psalm 34:18 *(for victim)*
Psalm 61:1-5, 8
Psalm 121
Isaiah 55:6-7 *(for abuser)*
Matthew 5:1-12
Matthew 7:7-8
John 13:34 *(for abuser)*
James 5:16 *(for abuser)*
Revelation 21:1-4; 22:5

Note: Full text of scriptures can be found starting on page 151.

Hymns

362	Help us to help each other
372	O healing river
377	Healer of our every ill
379	O Christ, the healer
418	Move in our midst

553 I am weak and I need thy strength
569 Day by day, dear Lord
596 And I will raise you up
1135 We do not know how to pray

Note: All page references are from *Hymnal: A Worship Book* or the *Hymnal Supplement*.

Notes:

Notes:

ILLNESS, INJURY, SURGERY

Prayer during a time of illness

Gracious God, your presence is such a gift to us. We thank you for being with us in this time of illness. We ask your healing touch to reach out to our dear *(brother/sister)*, *(name)* . May *(he/she)* feel your presence and your blessing. We give you thanks for the love that lives in this place. We give you thanks for *(name's)* family, for their care and support. We ask for healing, strength, and patience in Christ's name. Amen.

—*Christy J. Waltersdorff*

Prayer during a time of illness

O Sustainer and Friend, we are gathered together recognizing that your Scriptures tell us that where two or three are gathered, you are in the midst of them. We sense your presence here and now. As we are here in this place, we know that you are aware of *(name's)* *(pain/illness/unknown challenges)*. Together we ask that you hold *(name)* gently in the palm of your loving hand. May *(name)* sense your provision, and even now sense your infusion of strength. Even though we do not know what is ahead, Most Holy One, we know that we can rely on you. Amen.

—*Yvonne Riege*

Crises of Mind, Body, and Spirit 29

Prayer for someone with a serious illness

God who made us and knows every detail of our bodies, we ask now that your Spirit be with _(name)_ whose body is in need of healing. Thank you for the _(medicine/physicians/surgeons)_ available to *(him/her)*. May they assist your Spirit in the healing work that is needed. Allow _(name)_ to be patient if the mending should be slow, to be tolerant of pain and discomfort so that wholeness may be restored once again. Surround _(name)_ in your unmistakable ways, until this time is only a memory. By your healing power we pray. Amen.

—*Linda Alley*

Prayer for someone with a serious illness

O faithful God, you are our rock. Help our *(brother/sister)* _(name)_ to feel your steadying presence. *(He/she)* is reeling from stress and fear coming at *(him/her)* from every direction of life. Release *(him/her)* from the tension and fear binding *(him/her)*. Remind *(him/her)* there is a loving, supportive congregation standing with *(him/her)*, willing to help in any way. Surround *(him/her)* with your love, fill *(him/her)* with hope for tomorrow. In the name of the One who erases all fear, we pray. Amen.

—*Nan Erbaugh*

Prayer for someone with a serious illness

Merciful God, we are gathered here praying for our *(brother/sister)* *(name)*, fighting hard to recover from *(heart attack, etc.)*. Sustain *(him/her)* as only you can through the coming days of the recovery process. Grant *(him/her)* hope, courage, patience, and perseverance. You are the ultimate healer, God, and we put our trust in you. Amen.

—*Nan Erbaugh*

Prayer for the family of someone with a serious illness

Parent God, this family comes to you in a time of trial. They have faced their fears, and here they are with futures uncertain, dreams falling around ankles. We reach out to you in earnest, because we are running out of ideas. Help us to embrace what we do have—love, family, trust in you—even as other constants fall away. We ask you for patience, deep understanding, and hope. If nothing else, help us hold on to our hope, for without hope, we are lost. This family is fumbling now, in a world they thought they knew, and we come to you pleading for something to hold on to. Give them the strength they need to deal with diagnoses, changes in medication, and all the transitions forced upon this family. We are tired, and we are confused. In your name we pray, for hope. Amen.

—*Cassidy McFadden*

Prayer following a life-changing illness/accident
Read Psalm 46, and then pray:

God, you are our refuge and our strength, a very present help in trouble. Therefore we will not fear, though the earth should change, though the mountains shake in the heart of the sea, though its waters roar and foam, though the mountains tremble with its tumult.

We ask you now to be *(name's)* refuge and strength. *(Name's)* world has changed. It has been shaken; it trembles; it is in tumult.

We who were and are and will continue to be part of *(name's)* world rejoice that *(he/she)* is a part of our world! Help all of us to remember with joy the world that was, to celebrate that world with thanksgiving. Help us to hold steady in this world that is changing. Help *(name)* and each of us to believe that a changed world in this life is still a world in which we can find love and meaning, a world in which we will find your presence.

The psalmist says, "Come, behold the works of the LORD . . . . Be still, and know that I am God! The LORD of hosts is with us; the God of Jacob is our refuge." Allow *(name)* this day the comfort of stillness, in which *(he/she)* without fear, can behold your work of hope and help and healing within *(himself/herself)*. Be present to _(name)_ , a very present help in trouble. Enable *(him/her)* to know that you are God—the God of love who is a refuge in this tumultuous world. Amen.

—*Sonja Griffith*

Prayer for the illness of a child

Our Gracious Lord, we cry out to you this day. Lord, so often we don't understand the things of this life, but we take comfort as we claim your promises to us. Lord, your Son's earthly ministry sought out the little children. Heavenly Father, wrap your loving arms around _(name)_ . Fill *(him/her)* with your peace. Sustain this family and _(name's)_ life. God, we are so thankful that we can come to you in prayer. In the name of the Great Physician who still lives today, Jesus Christ, we pray. Amen.

—*Jeremy Dykes*

Prayer for a child with a serious illness and the family

Gracious God, we come to you sharing the pain of the _(Name)_ family. We need your healing touch both on _(name of child)_ and on _(names of parents or siblings)_ , in physical and emotional senses. This has been a difficult time, and the future is not looking any easier. They will need your loving hand and guidance through this time, with strength for hard decisions and also for many *(hospital/doctor visits)*. These parents need your parental guidance even as their children need theirs, especially in this time. God, please give everyone in this family the strength to carry on, but also the strength to cry out for help when they need it. This work will not be easy, but a cloud of witnesses to surround and support them is ready and waiting. In your loving name, we pray. Amen.

—*Cassidy McFadden*

Prayer of thanksgiving for healing

Come! Let us give thanks to God
   for the healing and wholeness
   that are ours through Jesus Christ.
Jesus brought good news to the poor,
   release to the captives, sight to the blind,
   and freedom to the oppressed.
Come and worship! For we are healed
   by the forgiveness of God,
      made whole by the fullness of life
   we know through Jesus Christ. Amen.

—*Sara Speicher*

Prayer before surgery

Heavenly Father, we pray that you will watch over our *(brother/sister)* during this time of surgery. We pray boldly for calmness and peace, for healing, for restoration to wholeness. We pray that you will bring healing directly to the body, through the action of your Holy Spirit. Knowing that you work through the hands of healers, we pray that you will guide the hands of doctors, nurses, technicians, and others involved in this surgery. Watch over friends and family both near and far. These things we pray in your Son's name. Amen.

—*Frank Ramirez*

Prayer before surgery or test (in hospital)

Merciful God, we are grateful for your presence in this place of healing. We ask your special blessing upon *(name)* as *(he/she)* awaits *(surgery/procedure/test)* . May *(he/she)* feel your loving presence in the days to come. We give you thanks for the care and wisdom of the nurses and doctors, and all those who work in this place. We ask your blessing upon each one. We give you thanks for *(name's)* family and friends. May they feel your presence as they wait. Thank you for hearing our prayers. We pray in Christ's name. Amen.

—*Christy J. Waltersdorff*

Scriptures

Psalm 22:1-2
Psalm 34:18
Psalm 46:1-5, 7, 10-11
Psalm 61:1-5, 8
Matthew 5:1-12
James 5:13-15

Note: Full text of scriptures can be found starting on page 151.

Hymns

372	O healing river
377	Healer of our every ill
379	O Christ, the healer
553	I am weak and I need thy strength
575	Precious Lord, take my hand
585	In your sickness
589	My Shepherd will supply my need
596	And I will raise you up
631	Anoint us, Lord
1135	We do not know how to pray

Note: All page references are from *Hymnal: A Worship Book* or the *Hymnal Supplement*.

Notes:

NATURAL DISASTER

General

O God, how powerless we are in the face of your *(wind/water/fire)*! Though this place is a small spot on your earth, the chaos seems overwhelming. Where do we begin? What are the first steps? Who do we help first and with what? Calm us, Lord. Let us find once again the still center. May we find strength there beyond our strength, wisdom beyond our wisdom, resources beyond our resources —a storehouse of all we need for such a time as this. Remind us minute by minute that we are not alone. Amen.

—*Linda Alley*

General

Dear Lord, rarely have we felt so confused, so harmed by life, so much in need of your love. Be with us now during this time when there seems to be no solution, no answer, only questions. Let your Word be our light as we walk through dark places. Let your Spirit be our guide as we walk through the valley of the shadow of death. Let your Son be our example as we tread uncharted regions of the soul. Let your creation be our assurance, even as everything falls apart around us, that summer and winter, springtime and harvest, will not cease. We pray in Jesus' name. Amen.

—*Frank Ramirez*

Prayer following a flood

Creator God, it seems our very lives have been washed away by the flood. We are straining to keep our heads above water, both literally and figuratively. We do not know where to start on the road to recovery, but we are so thankful just to be alive and together. Give us patience and energy for the long road ahead. Continue to remind us that you are with us every step of the way. In the name of the One who leads us to higher ground, we pray. Amen.

—*Nan Erbaugh*

Prayer following a tornado/hurricane

O Creator God, we are stunned, panic-stricken, and disoriented today. The winds went wild and now our homes are gone. We are heartbroken. Yet, as we sift through what is left of our lives as they were *(number of days ago)* , we are reminded that we are not alone. You are with us, always and forever. Give us strength to take the next step, knowing we can lean on each other as we grieve, regroup, and rebuild. A new day will dawn. Infuse us with hope, courage, and determination for the job ahead. Our rest is in you today as it was yesterday. In your holy name, we pray. Amen.

—*Nan Erbaugh*

Scriptures

Psalm 22:1-2
Psalm 34:18
Psalm 46:1-5, 7, 10-11
Psalm 61:1-5, 8
Psalm 121
Romans 5:1-5
Romans 8:31, 35, 37-39
2 Corinthians 4:5-12
Revelation 21:1-4, 22:5

Note: Full text of scriptures can be found starting on page 151.

Hymns

362	Help us to help each other
418	Move in our midst
557	Oh God, in restless living
569	Day by day, dear Lord
589	My Shepherd will supply my need
596	And I will raise you up
640	This is a day of new beginnings
1135	We do not know how to pray

Note: All page references are from *Hymnal: A Worship Book* or the *Hymnal Supplement*.

Notes:

RECONCILIATION

Prayer during conflict

O God, help us to see that we stand in our own way, preventing ourselves from experiencing peace with our neighbor. Help us to take the log from our own eyes, before we attempt to show others your way. Lord, take away our fears. Help us to look beyond the differences and see the things we have in common, knowing that we are all made in your image. Almighty God, reconcile us to you and to each other, so that we may bring your message of love, hope, and peace to all.
—*Terrilynn Griffith*

Prayer during conflict

Jesus, as we struggle through disagreements,
    remind us that we are all your people,
    that you have called us into one family,
    that you are not interested in our
        squabbles.
Let us come together in unity based on your
    lordship, not on our power.
Let us seek to be your servants first and foremost.
Bless us with the peace that passes understanding.
In your name we pray. Amen.
—*Frank Ramirez*

Prayer during conflict

God, help us to love each other as you love us. Remind us that no one is perfect, and that we can do more in this world by love than by any other means. Just as there is room in your love for everyone, so let there be room in our hearts. Amen.

—*Joy Struble*

Prayer for help with reconciliation process

O Perfect One, who knows all our thoughts,
> help us to truly listen to others when they speak.

Teach us to genuinely take time for those around us,
> and convict us when we aren't really there for those who need our listening ears.

Amen.

—*Yvonne Riege*

Prayer for reconciliation with an individual

Lord, it is not your will that the least of your servants should stumble. Nevertheless we know that all have sinned and fallen short of the glory of God. Now we ask that where there is brokenness, there might be healing; where there is despair, there might be hope. Help us to be the instruments of your peace. Help us to be the church for people who are hurting. Help those who are hurting to remember that you are with them.

We know that life is filled with little deaths and little resurrections. It is so hard to see ahead to the time when healing may take place. Bless now your servant who desires to be healed, who is one of your children, whose life is full of turmoil and doubt and despair. Bring light into the dark places of life, and hope in the middle of this trouble.

Preserve, too, all those involved in this brokenness, all whose lives are touched by disarray and difficulty. Teach them that your love is constant, fill them with the sense of your presence, bind their wounds, and carry them through the days ahead. These things we pray in your Son's name. Amen.

—*Frank Ramirez*

Prayer during a time of conflict within the church body

Lord, we struggle to regain our balance. Our church has changed. Some want it to be restored to the way it used to be. Some see possibilities in a new direction ahead. We cannot clearly see the way, but we believe you know the future. Guide us along paths that we now see dimly, in the way that you know is best. Let us not insist on our own way, but seek together your way. In the name of Jesus, who is the Way, we pray. Amen.

—*Linda Alley*

Prayer of thanksgiving for reconciliation

We imagine, Lord, that you are clapping your hands in delight to see walls between us breaking down, to see new paths from one to the other, to hear blessings instead of curses. Forgive us our sins against each other and against you, sins that caused deep separation and wounding. From this day on give us greater understanding, more ability to hear and interpret, more willingness to be first to show kindness, and a lack of interest in keeping score. Help us to walk together in peace. Amen.

—*Linda Alley*

Prayer of thanksgiving for reconciliation

And now, as we stand together
   and hold on to each other,
   may our strength be in our union.
May we be comforted by standing together;
   may we find courage to stand apart.
May we laugh and may we mourn;
   feeling weak,
   feeling restored,
   feeling nourished.
Brothers and sisters together,
   engaged in the dance of life. Amen

—*Steve Shelton*

Scriptures

Psalm 46:1-5, 7, 10-11
Isaiah 55:6-7
Luke 6:27-31
John 13:34
John 14:1-6
Romans 5:1-5
2 Corinthians 4:5-12
James 5:16
Revelation 21:1-4, 22:5

Note: Full text of scriptures can be found starting on page 151.

Hymns

336 When peace, like a river
362 Help us to help each other
418 Move in our midst
640 This is a day of new beginnings
1066 We meet as friends at table
1133 Christ be in my mind

Note: All page references are from *Hymnal: A Worship Book* or the *Hymnal Supplement*.

Notes:

3
TRANSITIONS

Transition implies movement, a change from one way of being to another. A specific event, a life-changing moment—anticipated or not—may initiate a transition, but transitions by definition take place over time. Each person experiencing a major life change will do so in their own way, and over whatever period of time they choose. As such, deacons should be prepared to offer support not just at the time a change first occurs, but throughout the transition. Support is often most needed weeks or months after a specific event occurs, just when the outside world has all but forgotten the initial event. With this, consider offering the prayers, scriptures, and hymns in this section often, even with the same person or family.

CHILDREN LEAVING HOME

Prayer for child and parents

Dear God, in this time of change and growth, help *(this parent/these parents)* to support and uphold *(his/her/their)* *(child/children)*, while saving also a place for *(him/her/them)* at home. Help *(this child/these children)* to be brave as *(he/she/they)* pursue new opportunities, to be strong enough to blaze *(his/her/their)* own trails, but also strong enough to call home for help when it's needed. We thank you for the time spent together and the memories made. Keep this family in your heart, even as they stretch across miles. In your name, we pray. Amen.

—*Cassidy McFadden*

Prayer for child and family

Creator of us all, you give us the gift of family to care for us when we cannot care for ourselves, to teach us the skills of life, to lead us along the paths of your way. As __(name)__ leaves this family for __(reason)__, may *(he/she)* carry with *(him/her)* the skills that have been learned and the discernment to use them wisely, along with the unmistakable knowledge that you continue to walk with *(him/her)* every step of the way. Guide, protect, and give joy for the journey. For those who remain behind, grant your comfort and the satisfaction of a time of nurturing completed well. They are experiencing changes, too, and we ask for your guidance as they move forward together in new ways. Thank you for the memories this family shares and will continue to build in the years to come. Amen.

—*Linda Alley*

Prayer for child and family

Loving God, parent of all parents, how hard it is when children leave home to live on their own. We think the day will never come, and suddenly it's here. Bless _(names of children)_ as *(he/she begins; they begin)* a new phase in *(his/her life; their lives)*. Fill *(him/her/them)* with memories that bring smiles and remind *(him/her/them)* that a new and wonderful relationship with _(name or names)_ has begun. In the name of the One who guides all ages and stages of life, we pray. Amen.

—Nan Erbaugh

Prayer for child and family

God of changing seasons, of endings and beginnings, of meetings and partings, thank you for your presence in every moment of life. We are grateful for a parent's guidance, teaching, and example, which has nurtured _(name of child)_ toward this exciting time. Be with _(name of child)_ as *(he/she)* encounters fresh challenges and opportunities. Divine friend, in all new experiences may your loving companionship be ever present. Encourage _(names of parents)_ to grow in a wisdom that smoothes the path toward greater independence. May the love that has long nurtured _(name of child)_ find new expression in growing mutual respect. Place in the hearts of all these your servants a deepened trust in you, that changing relationships and new challenges may be met with grace and faith. In Christ's name, we pray. Amen.

—*Mike Hostetter*

Prayer for new graduate

O Lord our Creator, we praise you on this glorious day. We celebrate as *(name)* moves on to another season of *(his/her)* life. We thank you for the special plan that you have for *(name's)* life. Your prophet Jeremiah reminds us that the thoughts you have for us are for peace, to give us a hope-filled future. The hope that *(name)* has, the hope that we all have, is in Christ Jesus our Lord. Bless *(name)* this day and, as *(he/she)* goes forward, may your hand guide *(him/her)* each step of the way. We ask all of this in the name of our Lord and Savior, Jesus Christ. Amen.

—*Jeremy Dykes*

Scriptures

Psalm 112:1-2
Psalm 139:13-18
Proverbs 14:26
Proverbs 27:11
Jeremiah 29:11

Note: Full text of scriptures can be found starting on page 151.

Hymns

163	Obey my voice
389	Take my life
395	Here I am, Lord
427	You shall go out with joy
517	Open my eyes, that I may see
640	This is a day of new beginnings
1058	Go forth for God
1078	I was there to hear your borning cry

Note: All page references are from *Hymnal: A Worship Book* or the *Hymnal Supplement.*

Notes:

Notes:

END OF LIFE

Prayer for a dying person

Lord, we try to count our days, but only you know the number. You give us life to enjoy as we do your work, and at the end of life we entrust our bodies and souls into your care. Just as you have been a faithful companion all along the journey, walk closely now with _(name)_ so that *(he/she)* may lean on you when steps are unsteady and the path is unclear. Assure *(him/her)* of your unending love and your unlimited forgiveness. May _(name)_ call on you at any hour of the day or night with certainty that you are the God who hears and cares. We pray in the name of Jesus. Amen.

—*Linda Alley*

Prayer at a time of unexpected death

Merciful God, we call on you in this time of pain and sorrow. We are hurting. Our tears do not cease. Hold us close in our sorrow. Help us to feel your loving presence among us in these days. We don't understand why death has come to our family. We were not ready to lose _(name)_. Give us wisdom and strength as we deal with our sorrow. Give us the assurance of your eternal love. Hold us close in these days of pain. We ask these things in Christ's name. Amen.

—*Christy J. Waltersdorff*

Prayer at the time of death of someone with a chronic illness

Gracious God, we thank you for the life of _(name)_ and all that *(he/she)* has meant to *(his/her)* family and congregation. We have learned much about grace from _(name)_ along the way. Even though we hurt deeply and will miss *(him/her)*, we are thankful _(name)_ is now free of pain. O God, it gives us peace to think of *(him/her)* surrounded by your loving arms. Amen.

—*Nan Erbaugh*

Prayer at the time of death of an elderly person

Most merciful God, we celebrate the life of our beloved *(sister/brother)* _(name)_ who has left this earthly realm. While *(he/she)* lived to be _(age)_ years old, somehow *(his/her)* death still seems too soon. We were not ready for *(him/her)* to leave us. May our vivid memories of _(name)_ bring a smile and sustain us all as we go forward. Comfort *(his/her)* family as they grieve. In the name of the Creator, Redeemer, and Sustainer, we pray. Amen.

—*Nan Erbaugh*

Prayer at the bedside of one who has died

We gather here in the protective shelter of God's healing love. We are free to pour out our grief, release our anger, and face our

emptiness. We gather here as family and friends, conscious of others who have died and of the frailty of our own existence on earth. We come to comfort and to support one another in our common loss. We come to remember and be thankful for _(name's)_ life. Be with us in these moments, and guide us through the hours and days ahead. Amen.
—*Ralph McFadden*

Prayer at the bedside of one who has died

Creator God, amid all the changes of life, you alone remain the same. We acknowledge the uncertainty of our life on earth. We are given a mere handful of days, and sometimes our span of life seems all too short—almost as nothing. Our hope is in you, O God. Even in the valley of the shadow of death, you are with us. Hear our prayers—spoken and unspoken—and turn your ear to our cries. Do not be blind to our tears in these days of sorrow. And lighten our hearts as we rejoice in the fullness of life.

We lift up _(name)_ before you this day. We thank you for giving _(name)_ to *(his/her)* family and friends, to know and to love on this earthly pilgrimage. In your boundless compassion, care for us in our sorrow. Give us faith to see in death the gate to your life beyond, so that in quiet confidence we may continue our daily lives, until, by your call, we are reunited with those who have gone before. Amen.

—*Ralph McFadden*

Prayer upon the death of a child or infant

Lord, we are fearfully and wonderfully made. In death as well as life, the complexity of your creation and the fragility of our brief time on earth are revealed. The grass withers and the flower fades, but your Word is forever. We come to you at this time, not looking for answers but seeking your comfort. We give back to you this life that was always yours, but the love in our hearts, which was planted there first by you, we hold to dearly. Abide with us in sorrow as well as joy. We do not ask to be freed from tears, but humbly seek cleansing from these tears so that we may see you more clearly. Let our cherished memories of _(name)_ remain clear and bright; let our hearts be set upon the work of your kingdom in this life as well as the reunion in love in the next. Thank you for the moments we have shared, and for your sharing in our sorrow. Our child was always yours and we commit _(name)_ into your keeping. These things we pray in both sorrow and hope. Amen.

—*Frank Ramirez*

Prayer upon the death of a child or infant

God of great things, God of small things, there is now a small hole in the universe, but there is a large hole in our hearts. We lament the loss of this child who has departed this life, but not our lives. These memories we cherish, and we pray that you will keep them ever fresh. We know it is not your will that even the least of these should fall, but our broken world is filled with sorrow. Even as you take this, our departed child, into your arms, we pray that you will keep memories green and undimmed as we go forward with you at our side. Great are you, Lord God Almighty. Nearly as great is our sorrow. Comfort us in our loss. Abide with us. These things we pray in your name. Amen.

—*Frank Ramirez*

Prayer for the family of a stillborn baby

Nurturing God, we mourn with you the loss of this child, *(name)*. We know that you have felt this kind of loss time and time again, personally at the death of your only Son and when you share our experiences of grief and loss. The suddenness is tragic and difficult to understand. *(Name)* didn't get a chance to laugh or cry or love, and we mourn for these losses, and for the loss of our time with them. This family, lost in a whirlwind of emotions, needs your healing touch. It can be hard for others to see how much of a struggle this is, but _(name of mother)_ knew this baby already, and the place in the family was open and waiting. We thank you for the love that is here to catch this family, even as they fall to grief. Please hold them in your palm, and keep them close in these times of pain. We pray in your name. Amen.

—*Cassidy McFadden*

Prayer following the loss of a loved one to suicide

God of strength, one whom we love is suddenly gone. We have more questions than answers. Something deep inside us is broken and hurting. Remind us that _(name)_ was perfectly known and understood by you, even in the last moments. Help us to trust that all of your children are within your sight and your care, always. Comfort us in this difficult time, we pray in your name. Amen.

—*Linda Alley*

Prayer following the loss of a loved one to suicide

God of mystery, God of hope, we pray now that you will heal our departed loved one, and receive your servant into your kingdom. We know that nothing is beyond your forgiveness. Strengthen us, draw us closer together, walk with us, and abide with us always. What is done cannot be undone, but neither can the bonds of love be cut. We pray for our own healing to come in your time. Amen.

—Frank Ramirez

Prayer following the loss of a loved one to suicide (Romans 8:31-39, adapted)

Forgiving God, we thank you for your amazing grace. If you are for us, who is against us? Nothing can separate us from your love, thanks to the actions of Christ Jesus. In all things we are more than conquerors because you love us. In this moment, we struggle with questions for which there are no answers. We grapple with situations for which there are no solutions. We face mysteries beyond our ability to solve. But we remain convinced that neither death, nor life, nor angels, nor rulers, nor things present, nor things to come, nor powers, nor height, nor depth, nor anything else in all creation, will be able to separate us from the love of God in Christ Jesus our Lord. Amen.

—Frank Ramirez

Scriptures

Psalm 23
John 14:1-6
Romans 14:7-9
1 Corinthians 15:50-55

Note: Full text of scriptures can be found starting on page 151.

Hymns

575	Precious Lord, take my hand
614	In the bulb there is a flower
637	When grief is raw
1120	Peace, be still, and know that I am God
1135	We do not know how to pray

Note: All page references are from *Hymnal: A Worship Book* or the *Hymnal Supplement.*

Notes:

Notes:

LOSS

Prayer for loss (general)

Help us, Lord God, to see the pain and loss that our *(brother/sister)* is experiencing. Help us to understand that we all experience loss in different ways, for different reasons, but that they are all recognized in your eyes. There is no loss too small or too great that you will not send your Holy Spirit to surround *(name)* as *(he/she)* grieves *(his/her)* loss. Help us to be grateful for your loving presence as we travel the road ahead. Amen.

—*Terrilynn Griffith*

Prayer for loss of a relationship

Heavenly Father, in this human experience it is hard to let go. It is hard to have, to hold close, and then to somehow feel that we must release this very gift. We know that change is a natural part of life, yet it is rarely easy. In this moment, we honor what has been. We give thanks for the blessings of *(name)*. We thank you for the joys this gift brought. Now, as we stand at the crossroads between holding close and letting go, we ask that you stay close to us, dear God. Lead us onward and remind us that in all of the changes of life, you are ever-present to help us move forward and to comfort us. Make a way for something new to come to

our hearts and our minds, that will not so much fill the gap, but refresh and encourage us to move forward. Give us the grace to turn to others when we find ourselves in need. We pray all of this in the name of your Son, Jesus. Amen.
—*Kathy Fuller Guisewite*

Prayer for loss of quality of life
Lord, we are so resistant to change, especially when we feel diminished by a loss in our lives. Remind us that we were created, first of all, to be in relationship with you. Help us to remember that our human doing is not as important as being in your presence. Let *(name)* experience an even closer relationship with you as old, familiar ways of living are limited. Keep the lines of communication between you and *(name)* open and clear. Bless *(him/her)* with the gift of knowing that *(he/she)* is whole and precious in your sight. Amen.
—*Linda Alley*

Prayer at a time of miscarriage or stillbirth
God of tender mercy, you understand our inner lives and silent sorrows. Before we are born you know us. With *(names of parents)* you shared anticipation and hope. Now, you also share their disappointment and grief. The loss of a new life weighs heavily upon

these your children. Sorrow brings with it
shock, anger, and a host of unanswered
questions. Divine Friend, thank you for not
deserting any who endure this pain. Just as
life and death are held in your gentle hands,
so, too, is the weakness and confusion of
these days. May the depth of their sorrow be
matched with the height of your consolation. Walk with *(names of parents)*, so that
they may be comforted and begin to look
forward. Through your deep love, O God,
kindle within them a strengthened faith and
a holy peace until a measure of healing
comes and hope returns. In your mercy, hear
us, we pray. Amen.

—*Mike Hostetter*

Prayer at a time of loss of financial stability

God of peace and God of plenty, you know
our every need. We come to you now, asking
for your loving presence to be with *(name
or names)* in this time of financial uncertainty. Hold *(him/her/them)* in your caring
embrace, and make real to *(him/her/them)* the
promise of your provision. God who cares
for the sparrows and clothes the lilies of the
field, we trust in your goodness and love. In
Christ's name, we pray. Amen.

—*Karen Allred McKeever*

Scriptures

Isaiah 40:28-31
Isaiah 54:10
Luke 6:38
Romans 8:31-39
1 Corinthians 13:3
2 Corinthians 9:6-15
Philippians 4:6
Revelation 21:4

Note: Full text of scriptures can be found starting on page 151.

Hymns

323	Beyond a dying sun
343	My hope is built on nothing less
1004	O God, we call
1060	God to enfold you
1081	What a fellowship

Note: All page references are from *Hymnal: A Worship Book* or the *Hymnal Supplement.*

Notes:

RELOCATION AND HOUSE BLESSINGS

Prayer for a move to a new home

We thank you, Lord, for the blessing of a new home to shelter this *(individual/family)*. May it become a refuge from the stresses of daily life and a shelter in times of trouble. May those who enter its doors experience the presence of your warmth and hospitality shown through those who call it home. The place *(he/she leaves; they leave)* behind is full of memories, joys and sorrows, friendships and companions, familiarity and comfort. Help __*(name)*__ to think of the centering and comfort that home provided, and use that centering to provide strength for the changes ahead and to offer hope that this new home will offer even more blessings. Go with __*(name)*__ as the Bridge between homes and the One who makes all things new. Amen.
—*Linda Alley*

Prayer at a time transition of moving to a new home and leaving a familiar church

O God of all times and places, __*(name or names)*__ *(is/are)* moving to a new home in another community. While we ache at the thought of losing *(him/her/them)* from our fellowship, we pray your blessings on __*(name or names)*__ as *(he/she embarks; they embark)* on a new phase of life. Moving can be so stressful. As *(he/she/they)* get settled in a new community, guide *(him/her/them)* as *(he/she seeks; they seek)* a new family of faith where *(he/she/they)* can share *(his/her/their)* many gifts. We pray in the name of the God who is present everywhere. Amen.

—Nan Erbaugh

Blessing when seniors experience a change of residence

O God, sometimes we resist change, and sometimes we embrace it. Change can be our nemesis and our hope. When we desire the change in our lives, we rejoice. When we lament the change in our lives, we mourn. God, *(name)* has experienced a change in what and where *(he/she)* calls home. And whether the change was desired or lamented, we know that change can be a challenge. We pray for the newness in this move to be embraced. Give *(name)* a sense of adventure and excitement for what might lie ahead.

We thank you, God, for the blessings in life—for the ways in which you do not change. We affirm our belief that you are always with us, the loving, caring, compassionate God who knows our every hope and every fear. O God, bless this new living space. May _(name)_ see the joy in the newness of change, and the possibilities that this move might bring to *(his/her)* life. We pray these things in the name of the One who walks with us daily.

—*Myrna Long Wheeler*

Housewarming prayer

Our God, how good and how pleasant it is to dwell together in unity. May the roof of this house be a reminder of your sheltering wings. May the walls stand strong as protectors against the storms of life. May the windows open to the light of your presence, and may that same light flow out as the doors are opened to friends and family, as well as to strangers. May the floors know the footsteps of many, and may each one find warmth and welcome. May your Spirit move like a cleansing breeze through every space within and take up residence here. May this house fulfill its greatest purpose as it becomes a real home. Let each one who lives here find rest within and a longing to return. May your peace abide here always. Amen.

—*Linda Alley*

Service of Home Blessing

Have family members and friends gather in the living area of the home or outside. Together the group will move from room to room. The leader will carry a small bowl of water and a stem of fresh herbs, such as lavender or mint. As the group moves into each room, a simple prayer is offered for the uses of each room.

Living room
Leader:
For those who relax and unwind here each day, may they find wholeness and rest.

All:
Come bless them with new life!

(Leader dips the herb into the water and sprinkles a bit of water from the end of it into the room. The group then moves on.)

Master bedroom
Leader:
For the heads of household who come here to seek rest and renewal, may they enjoy their time together.

All:
Come bless them with new life!

Bathroom
Leader:
For mornings when sleepy ones come here to wake and evenings when tired ones prepare for bed, may they sense God's love and care.

All:
Come bless them with new life!

Bedrooms of each child
Leader:
We thank you for the skills and talents of
 (name) . May this room provide space for creativity and learning, fun and recreation, as well as rest and sleep.

All:
Come bless _(name)_ with new life!

Kitchen
Leader:
For bread that nourishes the soul and drink that refreshes the spirit, give newness of life.

All:
Come bless them with new life!

Dining room
Leader:
For mealtimes of laughter and deep conversation, give willingness to smile and share.

All:
Come bless them with new life!

(This resource can be expanded for other rooms in the home.)

Stepping outside the front door
Leader:
For the impact this family will have on their neighborhood and community, give openness to share God's love and care.

All:
Come bless them with new life!

—Yvonne Riege

Scriptures

Deuteronomy 6:4-9
Joshua 24:15
Psalm 121:7-8
Psalm 127:1
Ezekiel 37:27
John 12:1-11
John 14:23

Note: Full text of scriptures can be found starting on page 151.

Hymns

6	Here in this place
38	The Lord is in his holy temple
504	Have thine own way
507	Gracious Spirit, dwell with me

Note: All page references are from *Hymnal: A Worship Book*.

Notes:

SEPARATION AND DIVORCE

Prayer for someone experiencing separation or divorce

Heavenly Father, we lift __(name)__ up in prayer today. Surround *(him/her)* with your loving Spirit as *(he/she)* faces this confusing and difficult time. Give *(him/her)* strength to make hard decisions and healing to mend the hurt and anger in *(his/her)* heart. Also lift up the family as they deal with feelings of loss and grief. In the darkness, you give us light. Open __(name's)__ heart that *(he/she)* might experience your Holy Light, even in this sad time. In Jesus' precious name, we pray. Amen.

—*Trinity Church of the Brethren deacons*
Sydney, Ohio

Prayer for someone experiencing separation or divorce, as well as the family

God of all love, this is not the "happily ever after" that we imagined. We come to you grieving for the relationship that is lost, and for the pain that both partners have experienced. We ask you to also comfort the extended family and friends who are affected. In the midst of every kind of brokenness in our world, we cling to your promise that you will never leave us or forsake us. Remind __(name)__ that you are as close as each breath. Provide strength for the changes ahead, we pray. Amen.

—*Linda Alley*

Prayer for someone facing a difficult decision

Loving God, touch *(name)* and help *(him/her)* feel your presence during these difficult times. Help *(him/her)* know that *(he/she)* is strong and capable and valuable to those who love *(him/her)*. Give *(him/her)* courage, strength, and wisdom to make the difficult decisions that need to be made. Amen.

—*Highland Avenue Church of the Brethren Transitions Sunday school class*

Prayer at the end of a relationship

It is difficult to look at the endings of relationships as anything but failure, but we know you don't see us as failures, O God. Help us to forgive ourselves for our parts in these endings, as you have already forgiven us. Help us to remember that these changes are not just endings, but also opportunities to let you transform us into people closer to who you want us to be. Amen.

—*Highland Avenue Church of the Brethren Transitions Sunday school class*

Prayer for a failed relationship

God of Grace, be with *(name)* in this time of so many changes. We try to model our

relationships after yours with us, and we fall short more often than not. Help us to learn and grow from our failings in relationships, and to make our future relationships stronger as a result. Amen.
—*Highland Avenue Church of the Brethren Transitions Sunday school class*

Prayer for a failed relationship

O God, you know the hurt that can come from a failed relationship: the sense of aloneness, fear, anxiety, loss, and pain. Be with _(name)_ now as *(he/she)* faces this transition. May *(he/she)* feel your presence, love, and compassion and know that *(he/she)* is not alone. Give _(name)_ a sense of hope and peace through your presence, and the knowledge that all will be well. Amen.
—*Highland Avenue Church of the Brethren Transitions Sunday school class*

Prayer for divorce or separation

Dear God, hearts are torn. How do we bear such a time as this? This is taking our breath away, and is taking a toll on everyone—the members of this family and all who love them. We pray for your grace, your comfort, and your healing presence. Hold out wisdom and send gentle souls who will listen deeply, souls who will extend compassion in the midst of this grief. Let love be the guiding agent in every decision and in every action of those who find that being together is no longer healthy. Place your loving hands upon each person, and whisper to them the words they most need to hear.

Thank you for the consistency of all things good—sunlight in the morning, seasons that follow one after the other, the freshness of rain, and the voices of friends. Let us lean upon such blessings and trust that in time, healing will come. May it be so. Amen.

—*Kathy Fuller Guisewite*

Prayer for divorce or separation

God of Witness, with you we heard words of pledge and promise, the sealing of a covenant with the words "till death do we part." These words were not lightly spoken, and as we come to a time when two lives are parted we recognize death. Lead us through death to new life. Help us experience resurrection in these lives. Forgive us our sins as we forgive those who have sinned against us. Open our hearts to new life, real life in Jesus. These things we pray as witnesses of a new beginning. Amen.

—*Frank Ramirez*

Prayer for the children of divorce

God of Shelter, God of Compassion, you have warned us that we should fear harming the least of these children. As adults we have made choices. These children have no choice, yet their lives are shattered, too. Shelter these children under your wings, and bless them that they may love and be loved by both of their parents. Grant that their dignity as your children will free them from becoming pawns or bargaining chips. Guard and guide all of us as a church family seeking your wisdom in difficult times. May we share the new life you have promised. We pray, trusting in you always. Amen.

—*Frank Ramirez*

Prayer for parents who have divorced

God of the Generations, God of History, our prayer is for these parents, our sisters and brothers, who were tied together as one family with one hope for the future. We are still one family in Christ Jesus, but the ties that bound them together have been dissolved. Now there is the care of their children and grandchildren, the hurt feelings, a broken covenant, and shattered dreams. You love us through all of this. May we continue to love each other, to support each other, to recognize in each other the marks of Christ. May we grow to experience together new life, new hope, and a strengthened faith, knowing that there is no place we can go where you are not present. Amen, God who sustains, and amen.

—*Frank Ramirez*

Scriptures

Psalm 6:6-9
Psalm 34:17-18
Psalm 107:28-38
Isaiah 61:1-3
2 Corinthians 1:3-5
2 Corinthians 5:17-19
Ephesians 4:31-32

Note: Full text of scriptures can be found starting on page 151.

Hymns

145	There's a wideness in God's mercy
504	Have thine own way
516	Just as I am, without one plea
1149	Change my heart, O God

Note: All page references are from *Hymnal: A Worship Book* or the *Hymnal Supplement.*

Notes:

Notes:

CAREGIVING

Prayer for caregiver

God of love and mercy, the source of our strength, our courage, and our abilities, grant *(name)* the skills *(he/she)* needs as caregiver to *(name)*. You taught us to love and to care for one another, and that you would equip us to do whatever is necessary in obedience to your will. We thank you for the privilege of this service and the love that motivates us to act according to your will. We ask for patience, strength, and courage in the name of our Lord and Savior, Jesus Christ.

—*James W. Hoffman*

Prayer for the caregiver of someone who is dying

Life-giving God, we pray today for our *(brother/sister)* *(name)*. *(He/She)* is a faithful caregiver and comes before you today asking for care for *(himself/herself)*. *(He/She)* accepts *(his/her)* caregiving role gladly, but needs rest and rejuvenation. Help *(him/her)* find reenergizing rest for mind, body, and spirit, the deep rest only you can give. Refresh *(him/her)* for the journey ahead. We pray it all in your holy name. Amen.

—*Nan Erbaugh*

Prayer for someone moving into a caregiving role

Dear Lord, we pray now for your presence, your wisdom, and your strength as we enter this next phase of life. May _(name)_ , our *(brother/sister)*, as *(he/she)* enters into the role of caregiver, never lose sight of *(his/her)* identity, nor of your love and support. Help *(him/her)* to take advantage of every respite offered, and to seek help when needed. Inspire us to go beyond simply praising this person for fortitude and strength, and instead help to carry the burden. Grant grace unto the *(one who is/ones who are)* being cared for, to accept with dignity and gratitude all that is being done on *(his/her/their)* behalf. The length of this journey, the twists and turns that lie ahead, the oases, and the landmarks are hidden from us at this time, but we know that you are already waiting for us at every corner. We place our trust in you, God of Care, God of Hope, God of Love. These things we pray in your name. Amen.

—*Frank Ramirez*

Prayer for someone moving into a caregiving role

At this time of transition we come before you, reliant upon you for guidance as we travel into uncharted territory. As our *(brother/sister)* takes upon *(himself/herself)* the mantle of caregiver, we pray for serenity to accept those things that cannot be changed,

courage to change those things within our power, and your wisdom so we may know the difference. Dependent as always upon your grace, we pray in your name. Amen.
—*Frank Ramirez*

Prayer for grandparent(s) preparing to care for grandchildren

God of Time, God of Patient Endurance, give our *(sister and/or brother)* strength for the task that lies ahead, discernment to know what *(he/she has; they have)* the strength for and what requires aid, courage to ask for help in this endeavor, serenity to abide in your love, perspective to perceive what is important and what is not, and joy always in the young lives placed in *(his/her/their)* care. These things we pray, trusting in your abiding presence. Amen.
—*Frank Ramirez*

Scriptures

Psalm 116:5-7
Matthew 11:28-30
Matthew 25:35-40
Luke 10:30-35
John 13:34-35
Galatians 6:2
Philippians 2:1-4
Hebrews 6:10
1 Peter 5:6-7

Note: Full text of scriptures can be found starting on page 151.

Hymns

362	Help us to help each other
553	I am weak and I need thy strength
569	Day by day, dear Lord
1133	Christ be in my mind

Note: All page references are from *Hymnal: A Worship Book* or the *Hymnal Supplement*.

Notes:

4
CELEBRATIONS AND MILESTONES

By its nature much of the work of deacons is reactive, responding to needs after something has happened. And all too often that "something" is not a positive event. With that, it's important that deacons are visible not only in times of need, but also in times of joy and abundance. As you shepherd those in your congregation, take the time to share all aspects of their lives. Celebrating birthdays is a great way to minister to children and youth; likewise, it's always appreciated when anniversaries are remembered, even those that aren't a special milestone. Brethren enjoy breaking bread together. Deacons should be prepared to offer meal blessings when asked, offering thanks both for the food and the many hands that brought it to the table, as well as for the fellowship itself. And what event holds more joy than that of new life through birth or adoption?

BIRTHDAY

Any age

Creator God, you breathed the breath of life

into Adam, and we thank you for that same gift, given to each of us at our birth. As we celebrate the life of _(name)_, we are thankful for your blessing *(him/her)* with that same precious gift. We ask for energy, health, and joy for the journey that is _(name's)_ life. May you be a guide and companion for *(him/her)* every step of the way. Amen.

—*Linda Alley*

Any age

Creator God, today it brings us great joy to celebrate _(name's)_ life. You made *(him/her)* wondrously! We thank you for the gifts and talents you have filled _(name)_ with, and for the many ways so many have been touched by those gifts. Thank you also for the ways we feel your presence through _(name)_. We ask that you bless *(him/her)* and continue to lead _(name)_ along paths of joy and peace. Let us never take the gift of _(name)_ for granted. Thanks be to God for _(name's)_ birth!

—*Kathy Fuller Guisewite*

Child or youth

Gracious Heavenly Father, we praise you this day for _(name)_. On this day you've given us a special opportunity to celebrate life. May _(name)_ grow in your love this coming year and may *(he/she)* continue to mature and become ever more like your Son, Jesus. In your precious, loving name, we pray. Amen.

—Martha Roudebush

Scriptures

Numbers 6:24-26
Psalm 4:7
Psalm 118:24
Psalm 139:13-16
1 Corinthians 1:4
Ephesians 2:10
Philippians 1:3-6
3 John 2

Note: Full text of scriptures can be found starting on page 151.

Hymns

85, 86	Now thank we all our God
486	God of our life
1078	I was there to hear your borning cry

Note: All page references are from *Hymnal: A Worship Book* or the *Hymnal Supplement.*

Notes:

ANNIVERSARY

Any number of years together

Lord, you created us to be in community. Today we celebrate one of the most sacred of all communities, that of the union of two people. We thank you for the gift of committed love, and for the many ways we learn patience, endurance, acceptance, and joy through the years we spend together. On this day of celebrating the anniversary of _(names)_, we ask that they may individually and together continue to grow into what you had in mind on their first day of meeting. Bless them with the sure knowledge that your kind of love endures forever. Amen.

—*Linda Alley*

Multiple years together

Eternal God, what a glorious time this is! _(Name)_ and _(name)_ have been married for _(number)_ years. Today we celebrate the depth of their love for one another. As that love has grown over the years, so has their trust in you as chief guide of their life together. Rain down blessings upon them as they continue their life's journey in you. Amen.

—*Nan Erbaugh*

Multiple years together

Heavenly Father, you have blessed this couple beyond anything they could have imagined. We thank you for being with them through the years as they faced the challenges of married life, and for celebrating with them in the joys of their years together. We give you thanks for the love they've shared over the past *(number)* years of marriage, and we praise you for guiding them along the way. We ask, Father, for your continued blessings upon this family as they strive daily to follow in your ways. In your precious name, we pray. Amen.

—*Loretta Sheets*

Scriptures

Ecclesiastes 4:9-12
Song of Solomon 8:7
John 15:9-17
1 Corinthians 13
1 John 4:7-12

Note: Full text of scriptures can be found starting on page 151.

Hymns

418	Move in our midst
421	Bless'd be the tie that binds
640	This is a day of new beginnings

Note: All page references are from *Hymnal: A Worship Book*.

Notes:

ARRIVAL OF A NEW CHILD

During pregnancy

How you must delight in forming a new person, Lord! Blue eyes or brown; curly hair or straight. Deciding where the dimples go, or not. Looking at the parents to choose a nose or a smile, or a particular tilt to the head or an unmistakable talent. We, too, wait with eagerness to see and hold, to know and love, this little one you are forming. We pray that even now your care and protection would be on this child, this mother, and this father. We pray that you prepare these parents for the adjustments they will make, and for the expansion of their hearts to hold a new supply of love. May this growing family find its center in you. Amen.

—*Linda Alley*

Birth

Once again, Lord, you have given us a miracle. We are in awe of your handiwork. You have allowed _(names of parents)_ to be co-creators with you in bringing _(name of baby)_ to life. We thank you for the safe delivery, and ask that you restore _(name of mother)_ strength for the tasks of mothering ahead. Allow _(name of father)_ to protect this child, and give both parents wisdom to model qualities worth imitating. Bless and keep this family—brothers, sisters, grandparents, aunts, uncles, and everyone—in your care for all the years and experiences ahead. We praise you for allowing us to participate in the wonder of this day. Amen.

—*Linda Alley*

Birth—for parents and congregation

O Great God, we rejoice today in the safe birth of __(name of child)__. Birth is such a miracle, an event we never take for granted. How very precious is this little one, and how very much loved. Shower your blessings on this family. Guide __(name of mother)__ and __(name of father)__ as they embark on the journey of parenthood. Help __(name of mother)__ and __(name of father)__ to trust in you, just as their baby trusts in them. Show us as a congregation how to provide loving support for this dear family. In the name of the One who made us all, we pray. Amen.

—*Nan Erbaugh*

Birth or adoption

Loving God, parent of us all, we thank you for the gift of __(name of child)__. We ask you to be with *(him/her)* as *(he/she)* grows physically and spiritually—may *(he/she)* always know your deep and abiding love. We ask for your blessing to be upon __(name(s) of parent(s))__ as *(he/she learns and grows; they learn and grow)* alongside this precious child. May this family experience laughter and joy as they embark on this new journey. We pray in the name of Christ, who loves the little children. Amen.

—*Karen Allred McKeever*

Scriptures

Deuteronomy 11:18-19
Psalm 139:13-16
Jeremiah 1:5
Matthew 19:14

Note: Full text of scriptures can be found starting on page 151.

Hymns

620   Child of blessing, child of promise
1063 Lord, we bring this child

Note: All page references are from *Hymnal: A Worship Book* or the *Hymnal Supplement*.

Notes:

Notes:

MEAL BLESSINGS

Lord, we are grateful for the food that allows us to continue to do your work. Energize us for the journey ahead, filling us with both physical and spiritual nourishment in our time together. Amen.

—Linda Alley

God of Abundance, you see our full table; fill our hearts as well. You see our full lives; transform them to allow space for your presence. You see our full homes; may they be storehouses of riches for sharing. In our plenty may we bless and share with those in need. In our need may we find plenty in you, today and every day. Amen.

—Linda Alley

Scriptures

Deuteronomy 8:6-10
Acts 27:35
1 Thessalonians 5:16-18
1 Timothy 4:4-5

Note: Full text of scriptures can be found starting on page 151.

Hymns

6	Here in this place
17	We gather together
52	Praise the Lord
1066	We meet as friends at table

Note: All page references are from *Hymnal: A Worship Book* or the *Hymnal Supplement*.

Notes:

Notes:

5
CHURCH OF THE BRETHREN ORDINANCES

When asked what deacons do, many in the Church of the Brethren are quick to respond: "They serve love feast." Participation in the ordinances—love feast and other services of communion, anointing, and, to a lesser extent, baptism—is certainly one of the primary and most visible responsibilities of deacons in the denomination. This chapter will include scriptural basis, history within the Church of the Brethren, and discussion around the current role of deacons in and for each of these ordinances, followed by practical helps such as prayers and orders of service.

In addition to the practical responsibilities of deacons as the ordinances are carried out, there is the equally important role of education. Deacons are often among those whom new attendees meet first and, as such, are in a good position to serve as mentors, explaining and modeling the unique traditions—including ordinances—of the Church of the Brethren. The introductions to the sections that follow—in addition to one's own experiences—will serve as good background to serve in all aspects of this ministry.

The Ministry of Anointing

> Are any among you sick? They should call for the elders of the church and have them pray over them, anointing them with oil in the name of the Lord.
> —James 5:14

One of the most powerful ordinances of the Church of the Brethren is anointing for healing. The scriptural basis for the ordinance is strong, especially as contained in the direct command of James 5:13-16. The ministry of anointing is also consistent with the call in scripture for petitionary prayer:

> "So I tell you, whatever you ask for in prayer, believe that you have received it, and it will be yours."
> —Mark 11:24

The Brethren's Church Manual of 1887 indicates that, in most cases, the minister will perform the anointing service; then it states: "Brethren, also, who are not ordained may administer it in case of emergency." These instructions are still valid today, as ministers usually perform the service, often with a deacon assisting, and upon occasion deacons may administer the anointing themselves.

Brethren Understanding about Healing

Brethren believe all healing has its source in God, and recognize that sometimes miraculous healing occurs that defies medical explanation. Generally, however, God uses human skill and wisdom to effect wholeness and healing. Medical and mental health professionals aid in the healing process, and their skill can be regarded as a direct gift from God.

Brethren believe there are several kinds of healing. Physical healing is often the most dramatic and the most visible form of healing, but there are times when emotional, spiritual, or psychological healing is just as needed as physical healing. Brethren believe healing is a *gift* and not a right. The prayer of faith is powerful, but the most faithful prayer was that of Jesus in the Garden of Gethsemane, on the eve of his great ordeal:

> "My Father, if it is possible, let this cup pass from me; yet not what I want but what you want."
> —*Matthew 26:39*

Anointing cannot guarantee healing; we do not control God's actions. It is God who invites us to become a community of prayer through the service of anointing.

If the prayed-for result does not occur, this does not imply a lack of belief or faithfulness on the part of anyone who participated. God acts freely and is not constrained or coerced. We believe that God will act from love and grace. It has been said: "Although a cure cannot be guaranteed, healing—as understood in the larger context of forgiveness, shalom, and wholeness—is the response of God in every instance of faithful petition." Healing is most effective when it becomes a gateway into a richer quality of life.

Those who participate in anointing need to be open to an unexpected and unexplainable manifestation of God's grace. Miracles happen at the time and place of God's choosing, and God continues to act directly as well as working through individuals.

The History of Anointing

The God of the Bible is a God of covenant. From God's promise to make Abraham into a great nation to Jesus' sacrifice on the cross, God has always been at work in people's lives—reconciling, healing, sustaining, and redeeming. The ordinances of the Church of the Brethren are all about these activities of God, and our responses.

Anointing with oil for healing is a covenantal rite. An examination of the primary text for the Brethren service, James 5:13-16, shows that a partnership is necessary for true healing to take place. That partnership begins with God who offers the possibility of healing and restoration; it extends through the church, represented by the spiritual leaders of the church, to the individual believer who by faith invites the process to begin. God's covenant is to love us, to forgive us, and to save us. The church, as the body of Christ, is the ambassador of God's covenant. The person being anointed participates in the covenant by turning to God in prayer.

The biblical expectations in James are clear: pray by yourself (v. 13), call for the spiritual leaders of the church and have them pray over you and anoint you with oil (v. 14), confess your sins (v. 16), and pray for one another (v. 16).

The call is to pray. Great and powerful things happen when we turn to God in prayer. It may not always bring us the cures we seek, but spiritual healing goes much deeper than our physical symptoms. Prayers of faith can save us.

Historically, the practice of the anointing service can be traced in the Church of the Brethren to the late 1700s, but there is every reason to believe it was practiced from the beginning of the Brethren movement. The biblical warrant was clear. Anointing in the Old Testament was reserved for special occasions involving the king or the priests, sometimes involving the renewal of the covenant between God and his people. The title accorded to Jesus, Messiah, means "anointed." Jesus sent out his disciples, charging them to cure the sick and anoint with oil (Mark 6:7-13). The early church continued this ministry. The letter of James gave a clear command to anoint for healing. In keeping with the New Testament theme of eliminating mediators and providing direct access to God through Jesus Christ, the new covenant of anointing was for everyone, not just for leaders. In this, as in other matters, Brethren attempted to imitate the ordinances they discovered through the communal study of scripture.

The Laying On of Hands

One of the components of the anointing service is the laying on of hands, often performed following the administration of the anointing oil. One or both of the officiating ministers places both hands upon the head or shoulders of the person who is anointed. Others participating might place their hands on the officiant's hands, or lightly on the head or shoulders of the person being anointed. Prayers are offered at the time of the laying on of hands.

Physical contact during healing was a part of the ministry of Jesus. Although he healed at a distance on more than one occasion, Jesus touched many of those who were healed (Matt. 9:18; Luke 4:40; Mark 16:18; Acts 9:12, 17). In many cases those who were ill had become social outcasts. The laying on of hands in the anointing service is an additional source of touch for those who need healing. We act as Jesus did.

Brethren do not believe that the action of laying on of hands ensures that physical healing or the desired answer to prayer will occur in all cases. Nor does something miraculous occur just because of the use of hands. However, this symbolic act represents the gift of the Holy Spirit. Those who lay on hands are the agents of God and represent the bestowing of God's love, blessing, and power.

Invitation to Anointing

In most congregations there is an unspoken invitation for anointing. However, ministers and deacons should also consider proactively offering the service of anointing to individuals in times of physical, spiritual, and emotional crisis.

One of the best ways to support the ministry of anointing—and introduce it to newcomers—is to make it a part of a congregational worship service. Anointing within the community may involve just one or a few participants, or the entire congregation may be invited to be anointed during a service.

If an individual chooses to be anointed during a worship service, the pastor or officiant invites the one being anointed to kneel or sit at the front of the sanctuary. Deacons, family members, and other special friends may join the one to be anointed, and indeed the entire congregation may come forward as there is room for all to gather around.

During the laying on of hands, deacons may place a hand on the officiant's hands or on the shoulders of the one being anointed. Others may put a hand on the shoulders of those closest, until everyone participating is in contact with someone else.

When anointing is offered to any and all present during a particular worship service, deacons might be stationed at different locations around the sanctuary. All present that day are invited to

be anointed; each may offer a word to the pastor or deacon anointing them as to the nature of their need (health, brokenness, a difficult decision, etc.), or they may remain silent. The pastor or deacon might use the simpler version of the sample anointing services that follow as the oil is being applied: "I anoint you . . .
- for the forgiveness of your sins,
- for the strengthening of your faith, and
- for healing and wholeness according to God's grace and wisdom."

To encourage others to participate in this ordinance, deacons might share stories that demonstrate the value of anointing. The church newsletter might feature testimonies from persons who have experienced physical or emotional healing through anointing. The pastor might be encouraged to feature anointing in a sermon or series of sermons.

Finally, deacons who are actively involved in the lives of the members of the congregation may recognize situations in which an anointing might be helpful. Brethren believe there should be no coercion in matters of religion, so some sensitivity must be used in the invitation. At an appropriate point, the deacon might approach the person by saying: "Have you considered being anointed?" or "Are you familiar with the Brethren practice of anointing?"

If the individual expresses interest, the deacon might share basic information about the practice, and ask: "Would you like me to call the pastor to arrange for an anointing?" or "Would you like to be anointed?" If the individual seems wary or worried about the practice of anointing, the sensitive and creative deacon will seek other ways in which the congregation can minister.

Preparation of the Individual for Anointing

Just as important as the actual anointing can be the preparation time, and deacons as well as pastors can be actively involved in that phase. Anointing may take place in the home, in the hospital, in the church, or at the scene of a crisis. While in many cases the atmosphere will be relatively calm, it is important to be sensitive to the condition of the person to be anointed. Extreme pain can mean relatively short spans of attention, and significant emotional suffering may make it difficult for a person to concentrate.

When the anointing service takes place at the home, the service will include certain components of a visit as well. Ask after the health and well-being of all family members, and invite spouses and others present to be anointed, if they so choose. The meaning and expectations of the anointing service should be carefully shared for the benefit of those present who may not be familiar with the ordinance. Then the actual anointing service should be described, and care taken so that the person to be anointed is seated or lying in a comfortable position.

The scripture is read (James 5:13-16 or other appropriate text; see sample services later in this chapter for scripture options) and an opportunity is given to the one being anointed to speak of any anxieties, worries, or sins that may be troubling them. The pastor and deacons may offer to help bring about any needed reconciliation in situations where a broken relationship might stand in the way of healing. The person might be invited to share a bit about the nature of the illness or trouble as well. As with all visits, this is a time to *listen* to another, not to offer your own thoughts or experiences.

It is important that the anointing neither be used nor described as a "quick fix" designed to minimize the suffering or the problem. Rather, it is an invitation to a closer relationship with God and the congregation, and a commitment to unity of body and spirit in accordance with God and God's will.

Special Situations

Although young children cannot fully appreciate the meaning of the anointing service, it is better to include children and to accept their level of understanding than to exclude them from the benefits of anointing. Even if the children involved are very young and have little or no understanding of the service, they can sense the peace and comfort extended to them, and to parents, grandparents, or guardians, in the anointing service. In any event, God is capable of responding to prayer, regardless of the understanding of any particular child.

The same is true in those instances when the person to be anointed is unconscious. Sometimes a person who appears unconscious is still able to hear and comprehend at some level. In addition, comfort is extended to family members through the anointing service. It is important to remember that God will be present, whatever the level of comprehension of the participants.

Among the Brethren, anointing is not considered a last rite, which is given by some Christian traditions to persons awaiting death. However, this is no reason to deny those near death the comfort afforded by an anointing. Those who have chosen to be anointed during other difficult times in their lives may wish to be anointed at this time as well.

In all of these instances, God's spirit moves among us as we challenge each other to remain open to that Spirit. God longs for our wholeness and health, and the anointing service provides us a means to seek God's healing Spirit.

Services for Anointing

Several sample services are available in various Church of the Brethren publications, including *For All Who Minister*. The services that follow supplement them, and may be more comfortable for lay leaders such as deacons to offer.

A Basic Service of Anointing

One or both of the following texts can be read at the beginning of the anointing service.

> The thought of my affliction and my homelessness is wormwood and gall! My soul continually thinks of it and is bowed down within me. But this I call to mind, and therefore I have hope: The steadfast love of the LORD never ceases, his mercies never come to an end; they are new every morning; great is your faithfulness. "The LORD is my portion," says my soul, "therefore, I will hope in him."
>
> —Lamentations 3:19-24

> Are any among you suffering? They should pray. Are any cheerful? They should sing songs of praise. Are any among you sick? They should call for the elders of the church and have them pray over them, anointing them with oil in the name of the Lord. The prayer of faith will save the sick, and the Lord will raise them up; and anyone who has committed sins will be forgiven. Therefore confess your sins to one another, and pray for one another, so that you may be healed. The prayer of the righteous is powerful and effective.
>
> —James 5:13-16

We are gathered together to anoint our *(brother/sister)* in the presence of God for __(reason for the anointing)__. We come boldly and with courage because Jesus commanded us to pray, "Give us this day our daily bread." We come meekly with fears like those of Jesus when he prayed, "Not my will, but thine be done."

Believing that, in the midst of a broken world, God wills your wholeness in body, mind, and spirit, I now anoint you with oil *(the officiant anoints the forehead with oil in the shape of three crosses)*:
- for the forgiveness of your sins,
- for the granting of peace to your soul (or "for the strengthening of your faith"), and
- for the restoration of wholeness to your body and soul.

The leader then places hands on the head of the person being anointed. Others present may place their hands upon the leader's hands or upon a shoulder, until all are touching. After the leader's prayer, a silence follows in which others may pray aloud or silently. The leader then closes with a brief prayer, followed by the Lord's Prayer in which all may join.

* * *

At times there may be little or no time for preparation. In those instances a single sentence may suffice:

  (Name) , I anoint you with oil for the healing of your body, the forgiveness of your sins, and the restoration of wholeness to your body and soul.
—Frank Ramirez

A Second Service of Anointing
Appropriate scriptures may be read as they relate to the present circumstances. Texts about Jesus' healing ministry or Paul's reminder that nothing can separate

us "from the love of God in Christ Jesus" (Rom. 8:39) may be used, along with the following text.

> Are any among you suffering? They should pray. Are any cheerful? They should sing songs of praise. Are any among you sick? They should call for the elders of the church and have them pray over them, anointing them with oil in the name of the Lord. The prayer of faith will save the sick, and the Lord will raise them up; and anyone who has committed sins will be forgiven. Therefore confess your sins to one another, and pray for one another, so that you may be healed. The prayer of the righteous is powerful and effective.
> —James 5:13-16

A prayer of preparation
God of grace and God of glory, on your people pour your power. We thank you for this opportunity to be together in Jesus' name, and we seek your guidance and blessing on what we are about to share. Open our hearts to receive what you have to give. In Jesus' name we pray. Amen.

Hymn
This is an optional part of the service. If the setting permits and the participants are willing, a verse or two could be sung a capella. Possibilities include (all are from Hymnal: A Worship Book) *the following:*

143	Amazing grace
327	Great is thy faithfulness
627	There is a balm in Gilead
614	In the bulb there is a flower

Invitation to confession and sharing
This is an opportunity for the person being anointed to offer their personal confession, or to give a testimony to their faith.

As far as you know, are you at peace with God, or is there anything in your life that you believe might prevent you from receiving the full blessing of God? Are there any thoughts or feelings you'd like to share, or would you prefer to pray silently?

> *Pause and let the person contemplate and share, aloud or silently. Don't be afraid of silence, and don't try to move quickly through the service.*

Assurance of God's forgiveness
Follow the sharing with reassurance of God's love and grace. Remember, God can forgive those things that are too deep even for words if we approach God with a repentant heart.

God is faithful and just and will forgive us our sins at any time when we turn to God with repentant hearts. May this loving God now bless us through this service.

The anointing
There are a variety of ways to handle the oil. It can be used directly from a bottle or "button," or a small amount can be poured out into your hand. From this source, touch your fingers to the oil and then touch

the person's forehead, and repeat three times, once with each petition listed below.

Upon your confession and affirmation of faith before God and these people, I now anoint you with oil in the name of Jesus:
- for the forgiveness of your sins,
- for the strengthening of your faith, and
- for healing and wholeness according to God's grace and wisdom.

Laying on of hands and prayer
After the third anointing, lightly place your hands on the head or shoulders of the person being anointed. If others are present, they can surround the person and join hands, with persons on either end laying a hand on the anointed person. Participants are invited to pray briefly as they feel called. When all are finished, everyone prays the Lord's Prayer together.

Benediction and departure
May the God of hope fill you with all joy and peace in believing, so that you may abound in hope by the power of the Holy Spirit. Amen.
—*Scott Duffy*

A Service for the Anointing of a Child
This service could be conducted in connection with a worship service of the congregation, or adapted to a family gathering in a home or hospital.

Introduction

Anointing with oil, especially for healing, has been used by the Church of the Brethren for generations. The faith expressed by this ordinance is based on the practice and teaching of the New Testament church, with particular attention to the letter of James, which reads:

> Are any among you suffering? They should pray. Are any cheerful? They should sing songs of praise. Are any among you sick? They should call for the elders of the church and have them pray over them, anointing them with oil in the name of the Lord. The prayer of faith will save the sick, and the Lord will raise them up; and anyone who has committed sins will be forgiven. Therefore confess your sins to one another, and pray for one another, so that you may be healed. The prayer of the righteous is powerful and effective.
> —James 5:13-16

We believe that this passage witnesses to the wholeness of individuals, to the interdependence of our physical, mental, and spiritual qualities. When any one of these is not healthy, the other two are greatly affected. Likewise, the health of any one part is contingent upon the other parts being as healthy as possible.

Anointing for healing is a means of sharing God's grace and blessing, intended to bring restoration of wholeness and health to the entire person. Normally, the anointing service is used with those who can express their faith in God and who are aware of aspects of their lives that need God's grace in order for wholeness to be effected. Today, however, we employ the anointing for __(name)__ because we are concerned for *(his/her)* health and wholeness and we seek God's blessing on *(him/her)*.

Jesus demonstrated his concern for children by taking them in his arms and blessing them. We also know through the testimony of the apostle Paul that God's power of healing can come through the prayers of those who call upon God's name in spirit and in truth. As we anoint __(name)__, we act as intercessors for *(his/her)* purification and *(his/her)* submission to the will and power of God.

The anointing

A drop of oil may be gently rubbed on the child's forehead as each of the following purposes is spoken.

__(Name)__, out of our love and concern for you, and as a symbol of our faith in the love and power of God for you, you are anointed with oil in the name of God:
- for the consecration of your life to God's will and grace,
- for the fullness of God's presence and love to bless you, and
- for your healing and wholeness according to God's will and wisdom.

Laying on of hands and prayer
Hands should be laid very gently on the child's head.

God of all life, in whose heart there is a very tender place for little ones, give to this precious one a full measure of your grace and power. We beseech you on behalf of *(his/her)* health, O God. Remove from *(him/her)* the *(illness, injury, etc.)* that is hindering *(his/her)* happiness and potential. And be near to undergird these *(parents, guardians, grandparents, friends, et al.)* with the assurance of your care, and with wisdom and strength for their vigil as they care for their little one. Enable the church, O God, to surround *(name)* and *(his/her)* family with the encouragement and love of Christ Jesus our Lord, who taught us to pray in common *(all pray the Lord's Prayer together)*.
—Fred Swartz

General Anointing Prayers

This section provides general prayers that can be customized to a variety of anointing situations.

For emotional healing
God, the events in *(name's)* life have led to wounds and scars, hurts and disappointments. Pour your healing oils down to soothe and soften, to cleanse and heal from the inside out, so that wholeness, health, and joy will replace all that is in need of your touch. Begin your transformation this day, we pray. Amen.
—Linda Alley

Healing

Gracious God, we gather as your people, trusting in your promise to be with us always. We seek your blessing now as we share in this time of anointing. In your name, a drop of oil takes on great significance and becomes a means of healing. We trust in your word and in your healing power. May that power now fill our *(brother/sister)*, *(name)*, as *(he/she)* seeks healing for *(reason for anointing)*. Bring *(him/her)* a sense of peace as *(he/she)* places *(his/her)* trust in you. We thank you for your love and healing presence. In Christ's name we pray. Amen.

—*Christy J. Waltersdorff*

For physical healing

God, we are marvelously made. In your wisdom you created our bodily systems to work perfectly, to interact with each other for our whole health and energy. We ask you now, God, to restore *(name)* to the kind of wholeness you had in mind from the beginning. Through miracles and physicians, through faith and prayers, through your healing oil as a symbol of your presence, open *(name)* to the deep peace found in resting in your hands. Take away fear of every kind. Replace it with the certainty of your presence, today and every day. Amen.

—*Linda Alley*

General
> As we enter into our time of prayer, I invite you to quiet your minds and hearts and pay attention to your breathing.
>
> With each breath, breathe in the peace of God.
> As you exhale, breathe out anxiety and stress.
> Breathe in the hope of God,
>   breathe out despair.
> Breathe in the grace of God,
>   breathe out harsh feelings of self-blame.
> Breathe in the love of God,
>   breathe out those fears that threaten to overtake you when the storms of life are raging.
> Breathe in peace,
>   let go of anxiety.
> Breathe in hope,
>   let go of despair.
> Take in grace,
>   let go of judgment.
> Breathe in love,
>   let go of fear.
>
> —*Joel Kline*

Anointing Prayers for Special Circumstances

This section provides prayers suited for special anointing situations, such as reconciliation, divorce, sickness, and preparation for death.

Anointing for reconciliation

  (Name) , you are anointed in the name of God, "who reconciled us to himself through Christ, and has given us the ministry of reconciliation." (2 Cor. 5:18).

  (Name) , you are anointed in the name of Jesus, who "is our peace" and has "broken down the dividing wall [of] . . . hostility" (Eph. 2:14).

  (Name) , you are anointed in the name of the Spirit, who empowers us to "be kind to one another, tenderhearted, forgiving one another, as God in Christ has forgiven" us (Eph. 4:32). With this anointing, symbolizing your innermost and highest desire for reconciliation, receive now in faith and reality, the gifts of reconciliation, healing, restoration, and peace!

—*Harold Z. Bomberger*

Anointing a divorced person

To be alive is to know the possibility of pain. Our *(brother/sister)* has come to know the pain of separation, of alienation. We believe that God wills for us health—of mind, of body, of human relationships. We believe, too, that all healing has its source in God. Living in this faith, we claim the divine promise of healing for our *(brother/sister)*.

(Name), you are anointed for repentance, recognizing that all of us have known and contributed to brokenness.

You are anointed for faith, that your trust in God's love and power may be confirmed and strengthened.

You are anointed for healing, that you may be restored to the wholeness of being that God wills for all his children.

—*Kenneth L. Gibble*

Anointing before surgery

(Name), you are anointed as an act of simple obedience, coming together before God and one another, claiming the process that wherever two or three gather in Christ's name, he is there in the midst of health-giving power.

You are anointed as an act of penitence, confessing before God and one another that we all together need the forgiveness and the wholeness made possible by Christ's forgiving spirit.

You are anointed as an act of petition, asking before God and one another that we be renewed in that hope which holds firm even in those moments when we echo Christ's own lament, "My God, my God, why have you forsaken me?" It is a hope that permits us to know that, even in the midst of suffering and pain, we have been

bound to God and each other by cords of compassion and ropes of love, which nothing in all creation can ever tear apart.
—*Warren F. Groff*

Anointing liturgy for a dying person

At this time we ask for God's mercy and grace to be made evident in death as well as in life. Recognizing that in each end is a beginning, and placing full trust in the risen Lord who said to a sinner, "Today you will be with me in paradise," I anoint you with oil for the forgiveness of sins, for clarity of mind and intent, and for the restoration of wholeness to your soul.

Let us pray.

Dear God, we offer to you this life, which was yours from the beginning, and which is now given back to you, the Lord of Life. We pray boldly for miracles, for wholeness and healing, and at the same time we pray for the strength to echo your son in the Garden of Gethsemane and say, "Not my will but yours be done." If it is your will that your servant and our *(brother/sister)* be called from this life, we ask that you give the peace that passes understanding to all present, and to all loved ones both near and far. Let your servant go in peace, for our eyes have seen your salvation in the person of Jesus Christ

our Lord, who taught us the words we now pray: Our Father, who art in heaven . . . .
—*Frank Ramirez*

Anointing persons or families suffering the loss of someone through death

(Name) , you are anointed in the faith that God, the author and finisher of all of life, will sustain you in the valley and the shadow of death.

You are anointed into the hope that God, who creates all of life, also re-creates life anew, transforming even death to life eternal.

You are anointed for the abiding love that God, who through Christ first claimed us, always brings into our midst. God's love will never let you go and will bind you together with all believing people as God's family.

Let this faith, this hope, and this love sustain you, and may God always be with you. Amen.

—*Robert E. Faus*

Anointing and commissioning for grandparent(s) raising grandchildren

Jesus said in the Gospel of Matthew, "Come to me, all you that are weary and are carrying heavy burdens, and I will give you rest. Take my yoke upon you, and learn from me; for I am gentle and humble in heart, and you will find rest for your souls. For my yoke is easy, and my burden is light" (11:28-30).

Caring God, this burden before us seems anything but light. The responsibility that lies before our *(brother and/or sister)* is great—but so is our joy. Circumstances have brought us to a place and time where it is necessary for *(this grandparent/these grandparents)* to take up the task of parenting once more. With this in mind I ask these questions:

To the grandparent(s):
Do you willingly take upon you the duties and responsibilities with regard to *(this young one/these young ones)*, pledging to raise *(him/her/them)* to the best of your ability, treating *(him/her/them)* with the love and respect each child deserves, and recognizing the limitations of age with regard to health and wealth? Are you prepared to reach out to this congregation for help in this endeavor, as God gives you strength, patience, and endurance?

We will.

To the congregation:
Do you pledge, as the family of God, to take up the joy of your responsibilities to present the face of Christ to *(this child/these children)*, and to be pillars of strength and encouragement for *(this grandparent/these grandparents)*?

Will you pledge not to wait until you are asked, but to actively seek opportunities for shared ministry and service in the name of Jesus?

We will.

Grandparent(s), child/children, and representatives of the church may be anointed in turn at this time.
I anoint you, *(name of grandparent)*, with oil, in the name of the Father, the Son, and the Holy Spirit, for the strengthening of body, mind, and spirit, that God may be glorified in our lives together.

I anoint you, child of God, as we prepare together to glorify God through the family prepared to take on the joys and challenges of parenthood, that you may be prepared to act in concert with all that is meant for the best of your welfare.

I anoint you, *(name of church member)*, with oil, in the name of the Father, the Son, and the Holy Spirit. May you keep eyes and ears open, so that words and deeds in due season may be offered for the strengthening and maintenance of this family, calling to mind that what we do—or fail to do—for the least of these is done—or left undone—for Jesus.

Let us pray. God, who calls all children unto yourself, we come before you asking for your presence, your loving kindness, and your endurance to strengthen this family, that we all may be ready to work together to raise these children in your name and for your service. These things we pray in the name of Jesus Christ our Lord. Amen.

—*Frank Ramirez*

Hymns for Anointing and Healing

The following hymns are suggestions when planning an anointing service. The hymns are taken from *Hymnal: A Worship Book*.

- 372 O healing river
- 377 Healer of our every ill
- 627 There is a balm in Gilead
- 631 Anoint us, Lord

Notes:

Notes:

Love Feast and Communion

> And during supper Jesus, knowing that the Father had given all things into his hands, and that he had come from God and was going to God, got up from the table, and took off his outer robe, and tied a towel around himself. Then he poured water into a basin and began to wash the disciples' feet and to wipe them with the towel that was tied around him. He came to Simon Peter, who said to him, "Lord are you going to wash my feet?" Jesus answered, "You do not know now what I am doing, but later you will understand."
> —*John 13:3-7*

> After [Jesus] had washed their feet, had put on his robe, and had returned to the table, he said to them, "Do you know what I have done to you? You call me Teacher and Lord—and you are right, for that is what I am. So if I, your Lord and Teacher, have washed your feet, you also ought to wash one another's feet. For I have set you an example, that you also should do as I have done to you. Very truly, I tell you, servants are not greater than their master, nor are messengers greater than the one who sent them. If you know these things, you are blessed if you do them."
> —*John 13:12-17*

> The Lord Jesus on the night when he was betrayed took a loaf of bread, and when he had given thanks, he broke it and said, "This is my body that is for you. Do this in remembrance of me." In the same way he took the cup also, after supper, saying, "This cup is the new covenant in my blood. Do this, as often as you drink it, in remembrance of me."
> —*1 Corinthians 11:23-25*

Brethren cherish the unique ministries of love feast and communion, ordinances that underscore our understanding that we are servants to each other as we follow the example of Jesus. Deacons can help faith communities hold fast to the gift of communion as Brethren practice it—employing the full love feast and feetwashing, not as something to be practiced symbolically by the few for the many but shared by all who will serve another and share in a common meal.

The love feast, including the practice of feetwashing, has been a consistant feature of Brethren worship throughout our history. Obedience to Jesus Christ is unchanging, and is both symbolized and manifested through adherence to this ordinance. The deacon body will want to take every opportunity to explain this service to others and encourage participation, as well as to tend to its preparation as a sacred trust and a joyful calling.

History of Communion and Love Feast

Deacons have been a part of the Brethren practice of love feast and communion for as long as the record can be traced. Traditionally, deacons have taken the lead in the physical preparations for these services.

The earliest Christian communions probably resembled the typical church carry-in meal, with individuals bringing food for the love feast. The genius of the early Christian movement was that its membership cut across all societal lines of division and disparity; the communion table was a rare focal point for equality. The earliest Christians remembered in their communion services not only the Last Supper, but the feeding of the 5,000, an event in which all ate and were satisfied. Representations of communion in early Christian art consistently include symbols of that particular miracle. For the poor of society, who rarely ate well, this sort of feasting was a clear foreshadowing of the kingdom as expressed by both the Hebrew prophets and Jesus.

Centuries later, as early Brethren read the scriptures, they sought to restore the communion service as a commemoration of the Lord's Supper as specifically commanded by Jesus. The elements in this restoration included an actual meal and the bread and cup communion. Furthermore, Brethren read in the commands of Jesus a clear message to wash the feet of each other following the example of their Lord. The complete Brethren love feast included a time of introspection and preparation, the fellowship meal, feetwashing, and bread and cup communion.

Today Brethren congregations generally celebrate the full love feast once or twice a year: on Maundy Thursday, the evening before Good Friday, and on the first Sunday of October, World Communion Sunday. Sharing bread and cup communion during Sunday morning worship several times a year is also a common practice.

Further information about the Brethren observance of love feast and communion can be found in *For All Who Minister*.

Preparation

Several weeks before each love feast deacons and pastors should meet to discuss the service and to delegate tasks. Practices vary from congregation to congregation, but most deacon bodies will want to determine who will help in the following categories:

- *Meal planning:* Some congregations offer similar, if not identical, menus for each love feast; others regularly vary the menu. Some congregations offer a simple meal, while others prepare more of a true "feast." As participation in love feast declines in many congregations, those responsible for its preparation might consider menu changes as a way to potentially increase attendance.
- *Meal Preparation:* How much and what food needs to be purchased, who will do the shopping, the advance preparation, cooking, and serving for the meal and communion?
- *Table Settings:* Who will set up tables (and when) and take them down afterward? Who will decorate and set the tables? What constitutes a place setting; which items need to be purchased or cleaned ahead of time?
- *Communion Bread:* Who will purchase items for and prepare the communion bread?

- **Feetwashing:** Who will prepare the rooms, towels, drop cloths, chairs, washtubs, and make arrangements for both handwashing stations and handwashing afterward?
- **Cleanup:** Who will be responsible for overall cleanup, including organizing it in such a way that all participants might do their part before leaving? Who will see that the kitchen is clean?

It's good to keep in mind, too, that while deacons traditionally are responsible for seeing that the logistics for love feast are managed well, it is not mandatory that only deacons participate in this work. Preparation for love feast is an excellent opportunity for intergenerational fellowship: ask youth to help with setup and food preparation, allowing them to see love feast from a different perspective. The physical labor involved also lends itself well to assistance from the developmentally disabled, many of whom are very pleased to be asked to serve in this way.

Preparing New Members for Love Feast

Persons who find themselves in a new country, or even in an unfamiliar part of their own land, fear that their innocent actions might be incorrect and embarrass them. It is always helpful to have a guide who can educate you about the local customs and often hidden assumptions before you make a mistake. New church attendees may feel much the same way, even during regular worship, and may be unsure if and when they should stand, sit, or kneel.

Add to such uncertainty this tradition called love feast, and the more unusual practice of feetwashing, and the importance of acquainting new attendees with what happens at a love feast service becomes clear. It is equally important to share with Brethren who have transferred from another congregation how their new faith community practices the ordinance as well.

Well before the service is held or even announced, deacons might contact new members and their families and arrange a time to talk with them about the service. It is important to emphasize in these conversations that Brethren practice this particular ordinance not as an innovation, but in obedience to the command of Jesus to do this in his memory.

Encouraging Participation

Lower attendance at love feast has been reported across the denomination, with reasons including: discomfort with the practice of feetwashing, decreased fellowship with the simplification of the meal, more members from non-Brethren backgrounds, lack of instruction and education and promotion, and taking the love feast for granted. And do not forget practical reasons like our greater mobility, hectic schedules, and more demands on our time, including that of our children.

Some congregations have reported making a concerted effort to improve attendance at love feast; when such effort was made, increased attendance in fact occurred. Consider the following opportunities, which might be initiated by the deacon body.

For Children and Youth
- Invite children at an early age to attend with their families to observe.
- Encourage parents to emphasize the importance of love feast to their children through teaching and example.
- Teach about love feast in Sunday school, vacation Bible school and other children's programs.
- Include a focus on love feast during children's time during worship, a week or so before each love feast.
- Include an emphasis on love feast in membership classes for candidates seeking baptism.
- Be sure youth leaders are committed to encouraging love feast participation.

Note: See pages 145-46 for more information on including children in love feast.

For New Members
- Include instruction about love feast in membership classes, including how it is practiced in your congregation. Discuss parts of the observance that may seem strange or uncomfortable—at times demonstration may be helpful.

- Assign sponsors to new members to answer questions and accompany them to their first love feast.
- Consider sending personal invitations to new members for their first love feast.
- Remember that new members may need time to feel a part of the congregation before being comfortable enough to attend love feast. Don't abandon too early the efforts to invite and encourage participation.

For Current Members and Attendees
- Encourage attendance through sermons.
- Publicize love feast through all possible channels.
- Announce love feast dates far in advance to allow people to make plans to attend.
- Offer to provide transportation as needed.
- Help members experience love feast as a renewal of their baptismal commitments.
- Invite inactive members to attend love feast.
- Consider holding at least one love feast each year immediately following a regular worship service.

Changes and Alternatives

Changes in the traditional ways of observing love feast, even if introduced with the intention of increasing attendance, should always be carefully made. When changes are announced, it is important to share how the decision was made and why. Whenever possible, a change should be offered as an option rather than as something that is imposed on everyone. For example, in congregations where men and women still sit at separate tables, family seating might be made available as well. If older adults or persons with disabilities find it difficult or impossible to kneel for feetwashing, offer handwashing as an alternative.

As mentioned earlier, changes might also be considered in the types of food served at love feast.

Although for many Brethren the smell, sight, and taste of beef is an essential part of love feast, for any number of reasons alternatives or a full change of menu may be in order. Remember that one of the reasons for love feast is the fellowship we are sharing as we remember Jesus' commandment that we do this and remember him; the menu itself is secondary.

Alternative menus might include the following:
- Fruit, cheese, and bread
- Soup, bread, and fruit
- Fruit, raw vegetables, hummus, and bread
- Rice and beans, fruit, and bread

In these and in other issues related to love feast, the goal is to welcome and to include; if a particular menu or custom will exclude some attendees, alternatives should be considered.

Worship Resources for Love Feast

A variety of resources are given here for deacons' use as they provide leadership in the love feast service. Other materials can be found in *For All Who Minister*.

Meditation for the Feetwashing Service
Read John 13:1-17, followed by the following meditation.

It doesn't matter where you live, you become comfortable with certain customs or ways that are part of your background, your family, your tradition. It wasn't any different in Jesus' day. It was the custom of servants to wash the tired, dirty feet of guests as they entered a home. It would have been terrible not to provide this gesture of welcome and hospitality.

The scene in this scripture is a familiar one to Brethren. The disciples have prepared this special meal in a room, all according to Jesus' instructions. As they gather for the meal, they are debating, even arguing, about who would sit next to Jesus and who would be first or greatest in his coming kingdom. Within the shadow of the cross, even after three years of teaching, they still don't understand. The problem was that whenever there was a question about who was the greatest, there was also much concern over who was the least. After all, it was only the least—the servants—who washed others' feet, and no one wanted to be seen as the least!

Can you imagine the scene in the Upper Room? The disciples are debating, arguing, waiting for someone to be the servant. The basin, towel, and water are ready, but no one steps forth. In the midst of this uneasiness, Jesus slowly rises, and without one word of explanation, girds himself with a towel, stoops down, and begins to wash his disciples' feet.

Peter—bold, outspoken Peter—speaks the words that everyone is thinking: "Lord, are you going to wash my feet? You will never wash my feet." Jesus completes his servant act of feetwashing and then sits down to explain what he has done. This feetwashing is meant for a different kind of cleaning, inner cleansing of the soul. Jesus was trying once again to show that there is only one kind of greatness, the greatness of service. We need to kneel at the feet of our brothers and sisters, washing their feet as a sign of service, humility, and inner cleansing.

Feetwashing symbolizes the continuance of our cleansing initially received at baptism. It is a time for us to be reminded of our sins and also to be reminded that we are cleansed.

All of us have heard of Mother Teresa and her many years of loving service to those in need. She told the story of a new helper, called out of a real sense of urgency to help others. However, when this new helper saw the deep and infected wounds of her next patient, she refused to clean his wounds. Maggots were crawling in and round them, and she said, "I can't do it! I can't cleanse his wounds." Mother Teresa gently answered, "Yes, you can! Yes, you can! Just picture that you are cleaning the wounds of Jesus."

What does feetwashing mean to each of us? How can it prepare us for the real world? How is it relevant to our faith? Jesus said, "So if I, your Lord and Teacher, have washed your feet, you also ought to wash one another's feet. For I have set you an example, that you also should do as I have done to you . . . . If you know these things, you are blessed if you do them."

May our eyes be opened to a new understanding of Christ's love as we share in this experience of feetwashing.

—S. Joan Hershey

A Call to Worship for Love Feast
Leader:
Jesus says . . . "Take and eat," calling us to share in his life.

People:
An invitation to intimacy, to love, to communion.

Leader:
Jesus says . . . "My burden is light," calling us to a journey of discipleship.

People:
An invitation to follow, to learn, to grow.

Leader:
Jesus says . . . "Even unto the least of these," calling us to compassion.

People:
An invitation to do justice, to walk the way of peace.

Leader:
Jesus says . . . "Like a mustard seed," calling us to look for the kingdom.

People:
An invitation to experience God in our midst, here in this moment.

—*Mark Flora Swick*

Prayer for the Love Feast Meal
Eternal God, giver and sustainer of life, we sense your almighty presence in these sacred moments. We offer our thanks and praise for your invitation to each of us to be present around these tables.

As we share in this fellowship meal, make us mindful of that table—almost 2,000 years ago—where our Lord and Savior ate with his disciples. We, like them, do not always understand your teachings; and those we do understand, we too often fail to follow.

Stir our hearts to obedience, an obedience that springs forth from a heart full of devotion for you. Move in our midst, touch our hands, transform our darkness into your light; but most of all, teach us to love you with our hearts, souls, and minds. O Spirit of God, lead us this night. In Christ's name we pray. Amen.

—S. Joan Hershey

A Liturgy for the Fellowship Meal

This liturgy is a responsive reading from the Didache, an early church manual with materials dating back to AD 60. It has been translated from the original Greek. The text from this manual for bread and cup communion is provided below.

Leader:
And regarding the thanksgiving [eucharist], give thanks in this way. Regarding first the cup—we give thanks to you, our Father, for the holy vine of your servant David, which you revealed fully in Jesus your servant.

All:
Glory to you forever.

Leader:
And regarding the broken bread—we give thanks to you, our Father, for the life and the knowledge which you have made known to us through your servant Jesus.

All:
Glory to you forever.

Leader:
For as this bread was once scattered over the

mountains but was brought together into one loaf, so too gather your fellowship from the four corners of the world into your kingdom.

All:
For yours are the glory and the power through Jesus Christ, forever.

The meal then follows. The Didache gives the following instructions for after the meal: "This is how you should give thanks after everyone is full."

Leader:
Holy Father, we give thanks to you for your holy name, which you have planted in our hearts, and for the knowledge and faith and eternal life you have made known through Jesus your servant.

All:
Glory to you forever.

Leader:
All powerful ruler, who made everything with your name in mind, you gave people food and drink to make us glad so they could thank you for it. And to us you have given spiritual food and drink, and eternal life, through your servant Jesus. We thank you most of all for being all-powerful.

All:
Glory to you forever.

Leader:
Remember your church, Lord, and preserve it

from evil, perfecting it in your love, and gathering it from the four winds, in holiness, into your kingdom which you have prepared for it.

All:
For yours is the power and the glory, forever.

Leader:
Let your grace come, let this world pass away.

All:
Hosanna to the son of David.

Leader:
If anyone is holy, let them approach. If anyone is not, let them repent. Maranatha—come soon, Lord. Amen.

—*Frank Ramirez*

A Meditation on the Agape Meal

In the spirit of Christ and in acceptance of each other, we eat this meal together. We pour out our hearts in gratitude, and we grieve for those who have no food, no table of love, no spiritual family.

We are guests at these tables this evening, and Jesus Christ is our host. As followers of our Lord, we have an opportunity to sit at the most extraordinary table that has ever been prepared. It is the oldest table in the world—it has been spread continuously for almost 2,000 years. It is the longest table, extending around the world. It is the widest table, including all believers who will come.

The love feast brings the Upper Room into our own experience as we remember what happened that night. It was during supper that Jesus gave his disciples one commandment, namely that they should have the same love for one another that he had for them. We know that there is nothing greater in all the world than his love for us. When we gather as believers to celebrate this feast, it becomes a beautiful memorial to his love.

Eating together has always been an act of friendliness and love. We come here in the Spirit of Christ and in acceptance of each other. We have not come to think on ourselves, but rather on Jesus Christ, who through his death and resurrection rescued us from the power of sin and death. Christ calls us to these tables as his followers and members of one body.

The very realization that we can share so much love in these moments should bring us to tears. But, it also brings us to action. We must reach out to those who have no physical or spiritual food, who have not experienced acceptance and love around a table, who have been robbed of the blessings of a spiritual family. We should be sentenced as guilty when it comes to embracing those who are missing from our tables because of our indifference, our selfishness, our greed.

As we eat in silence may our spirits be quickened by the Holy Spirit with a deeper dimension of gratitude, and may we be so filled that we will burst forth from this place with a zeal for others that knows no boundaries except Christ's love.

—*S. Joan Hershey*

Hymns for Love Feast and Communion
The following hymns, appropriate for different parts of love feast, are all from *Hymnal: A Worship Book* or the *Hymnal Supplement*.

Gathering
8	Brethren, we have met to worship
17	We gather together

Feetwashing
449	Jesus took a towel
450	Here in our upper room
1065	Jesu, Jesu, fill us with your love

Communion
453	Let us break bread together
454	Seed, scattered and sown
457	Be present at our table, Lord
463	Let all mortal flesh keep silence
471	Eat this bread

Closing
421	Bless'd be the tie that binds
430	God be with you
478	Sent forth by God's blessing

Inclusion of Children in Love Feast

While some congregations limit participation to members, in effect excluding most children, most encourage some participation to familiarize children with the love feast. This may include the opportunity to observe the service, and perhaps to partake of the meal. One congregation includes children at the love feast tables and provides crackers and apple juice for them in place of the bread and cup.

Others in the Church of the Brethren believe that all are called to the Lord's Table, noting that at the Last Supper even Judas Iscariot was present, and that in another context Jesus insisted that children, who in his day were marginalized persons of little worth, be brought to him for blessing. They also suggest that although children cannot appreciate the love feast at the same level as those who have made a commitment to Christ, it is a mistake to exclude them; they will understand what is happening at their own level. From this faith understanding, some congregations allow children fuller participation in the love feast service.

Bread and Cup Communion

Most Brethren congregations join with other Christian traditions in celebrating bread and cup communion, apart from the full love feast, several times a year. The role of deacons will vary based on congregational tradition, but it will almost always be a significant role. To that end, deacons are encouraged to plan for each bread and cup communion service similarly to love feast so that all responsibilities are appropriately delegated and cared for.

Notes:

Believers Baptism

> And Jesus came and said to them, "All authority in heaven and on earth has been given to me. Go therefore and make disciples of all nations, baptizing them in the name of the Father and of the Son and of the Holy Spirit, and teaching them to obey everything that I have commanded you. And remember, I am with you always, to the end of the age."
>
> —Matthew 28:18-20

Before making any serious commitment, a person considers the meaning behind and consequences of that choice. Often, he or she undergoes a public ceremony to acknowledge the momentous personal decision. For Brethren, the ordinance of believers baptism marks just such a deliberate, thoughtful commitment.

Choosing to follow the example of Jesus begins with repenting, or humbly reexamining one's relationship with God. Jesus himself showed us the way. In Mark 1:9-11 he asked to be baptized by John, and later he instructed his disciples to baptize others who wanted to be symbolically "reborn" through God's grace, into a new life of mature belief and service (cf. Matt. 28:16-20; Acts 2:37-42).

Over three hundred years ago, the first Brethren chose adult baptism as their ceremonial response to God's saving act—the life, death, and resurrection of Jesus Christ. Today, in the presence of the congregation, a newly committed person kneels in the water of the baptistry, publicly acknowledges his or her decision, and is immersed three times forward, "in the name of the Father and of the Son and of the Holy Spirit."

Through this symbolic cleansing and rebirth, the person becomes a full member of the Brethren congregation and of the larger body of Christ. The decision to be baptized indicates a willingness to take on both the joy and the responsibility of living Jesus' teachings.

The Role of Deacons in Baptism

The role of congregational deacons in baptism is usually much more limited than with the other ordinances, as ordained pastors generally conduct the full service. Deacons should make themselves available as needed, of course, to assist with things like helping those being baptized in and out of the water, offering towels, and other logistical tasks.

Just as with the other ordinances, deacons can play a key role in helping new attendees understand the concept of believers baptism, as many coming into the faith community may have been baptized as infants.

Notes:

Full List of Scriptures

This appendix provides the full text for scriptures listed in chapters 2 through 4. They are organized in the order they appear in the Bible. The scriptures come from *The New Revised Standard Version*, unless otherwise noted. Some familiar scriptures, such as Psalm 23 and John 3:16, are given in the King James Version, which was a translation lauded for its poetical nature and used by many when memorizing and studying scripture. Other modern translations or paraphrases are noted where used.

Numbers 6:24-26
The Lord bless you and keep you;
>   the Lord make his face to shine upon you,
>   and be gracious to you;
>   the Lord lift up his countenance upon you,
>   and give you peace.

So they shall put my name on the Israelites,
>   and I will bless them.

Deuteronomy 6:4-9
Hear, O Israel: The Lord is our God, the Lord alone. You shall love the Lord your God with all your heart, and with all your soul, and with all your might. Keep these words that I am commanding you today in your heart. Recite them to

your children and talk about them when you are at home and when you are away, when you lie down and when you rise. Bind them as a sign on your hand, fix them as an emblem on your forehead, and write them on the doorposts of your house and on your gates.

Deuteronomy 8:6-10
Therefore keep the commandments of the Lord your God, by walking in his ways and by fearing him. For the Lord your God is bringing you into a good land, a land with flowing streams, with springs and underground waters welling up in valleys and hills, a land of wheat and barley, of vines and fig trees and pomegranates, a land of olive trees and honey, a land where you may eat bread without scarcity, where you will lack nothing, a land whose stones are iron and from whose hills you may mine copper. You shall eat your fill and bless the Lord your God for the good land that he has given you.

Joshua 24:15
"Now if you are unwilling to serve the Lord, choose this day whom you will serve, whether the gods your ancestors served in the region beyond the River or the gods of the Amorites in whose land you are living; but as for me and my household, we will serve the Lord."

Psalm 4:7
You have put gladness in my heart
> more than when their grain and wine abound.

Psalm 6:6-9
I am weary with my moaning;
> every night I flood my bed with tears;
> I drench my couch with my weeping.

My eyes waste away because of grief;
> they grow weak because of all my foes.

Depart from me, all you workers of evil,
> for the Lord has heard the sound of my
>> weeping.

The Lord has heard my supplication;
> the Lord accepts my prayer.

Psalm 22:1-2
My God, my God, why have you forsaken me?
> Why are you so far from helping me, from the
>> words of my groaning?

O my God, I cry by day, but you do not answer;
> and by night, but find no rest.

Psalm 23, *King James Version*
The Lord is my shepherd; I shall not want.
He maketh me to lie down in green pastures:
> he leadeth me beside the still waters.

He restoreth my soul:
> he leadeth me in the paths
> of righteousness for his name's sake.

Yea, though I walk through the valley of the
> shadow of death, I will fear no evil:
>> for thou art with me; thy rod and thy staff
>>> they comfort me.
Thou preparest a table before me in the presence
> of mine enemies:
>> thou anointest my head with oil; my cup
>>> runneth over.
Surely goodness and mercy shall follow me all
> the days of my life:
>> and I will dwell in the house of the Lord
>>> for ever.

Psalm 25:1-10
To you, O Lord, I lift up my soul.
O my God, in you I trust;
> do not let me be put to shame;
> do not let my enemies exult over me.
Do not let those who wait for you be put to
> shame;
>> let them be ashamed who are wantonly
>>> treacherous.
Make me to know your ways, O Lord;
> teach me your paths.
Lead me in your truth, and teach me,
> for you are the God of my salvation;
> for you I wait all day long.
Be mindful of your mercy, O Lord, and of your
> steadfast love,
>> for they have been from of old.

Do not remember the sins of my youth or my
> transgressions;
>> according to your steadfast love remember
>> me,
>> for your goodness' sake, O Lord!
Good and upright is the Lord;
> therefore he instructs sinners in the way.
He leads the humble in what is right,
> and teaches the humble his way.
All the paths of the Lord are steadfast love and
> faithfulness,
>> for those who keep his covenant and his
>> decrees.

Psalm 34:17-18
When the righteous cry for help, the Lord hears,
> and rescues them from all their troubles.
The Lord is near to the brokenhearted,
> and saves the crushed in spirit.

Psalm 46:1-5, 7, 10-11
God is our refuge and strength,
> a very present help in trouble.
Therefore we will not fear, though the earth
> should change,
>> though the mountains shake in the heart of
>> the sea;
though its waters roar and foam,
> though the mountains tremble with its
> tumult.

There is a river whose streams make glad the city
    of God,
    the holy habitation of the Most High.
God is in the midst of the city; it shall not be
    moved;
    God will help it when the morning dawns. . . .
The LORD of hosts is with us;
    the God of Jacob is our refuge. . . .
"Be still, and know that I am God!
    I am exalted among the nations,
    I am exalted in the earth."
The LORD of hosts is with us;
    the God of Jacob is our refuge.

Psalm 61:1-5, 8
Hear my cry, O God;
    listen to my prayer.
From the end of the earth I call to you,
    when my heart is faint.
Lead me to the rock
    that is higher than I;
for you are my refuge,
    a strong tower against the enemy.
Let me abide in your tent forever,
    find refuge under the shelter of your wings.
For you, O God, have heard my vows;
    you have given me the heritage of those who
        fear your name. . . .
So I will always sing praises to your name,
    as I pay my vows day after day.

Psalm 107:28-38
Then they cried to the Lord in their trouble,
>and he brought them out from their distress;
he made the storm be still,
>and the waves of the sea were hushed.
Then they were glad because they had quiet,
>and he brought them to their desired haven.
Let them thank the Lord for his steadfast love,
>for his wonderful works to humankind.
Let them extol him in the congregation of the people,
>and praise him in the assembly of the elders.
He turns rivers into a desert,
>springs of water into thirsty ground,
a fruitful land into a salty waste,
>because of the wickedness of its inhabitants.
He turns a desert into pools of water,
>a parched land into springs of water.
And there he lets the hungry live,
>and they establish a town to live in;
they sow fields, and plant vineyards,
>and get a fruitful yield.
By his blessing they multiply greatly,
>and he does not let their cattle decrease.

Psalm 112:1-2
Praise the Lord!
>Happy are those who fear the Lord,
>who greatly delight in his commandments.
Their descendants will be mighty in the land;
>the generation of the upright will be blessed.

Psalm 116:5-7
Gracious is the Lord, and righteous;
>our God is merciful.
The Lord protects the simple;
>when I was brought low, he saved me.
Return, O my soul, to your rest,
>for the Lord has dealt bountifully with you.

Psalm 118:24
This is the day that the Lord has made;
>let us rejoice and be glad in it.

Psalm 119:105-112
Your word is a lamp to my feet
>and a light to my path.
I have sworn an oath and confirmed it,
>to observe your righteous ordinances.
I am severely afflicted;
>give me life, O Lord, according to your word.
Accept my offerings of praise, O Lord,
>and teach me your ordinances.
I hold my life in my hand continually,
>but I do not forget your law.
The wicked have laid a snare for me,
>but I do not stray from your precepts.
Your decrees are my heritage forever;
>they are the joy of my heart.
I incline my heart to perform your statutes
>forever, to the end.

Psalm 121

I lift up my eyes to the hills—
> from where will my help come?

My help comes from the Lord,
> who made heaven and earth.

He will not let your foot be moved;
> he who keeps you will not slumber.

He who keeps Israel
> will neither slumber nor sleep.

The Lord is your keeper;
> the Lord is your shade at your right hand.

The sun shall not strike you by day,
> nor the moon by night.

The Lord will keep you from all evil;
> he will keep your life.

The Lord will keep
> your going out and your coming in
> from this time on and forevermore.

Psalm 127:1

Unless the Lord builds the house,
> those who build it labor in vain.

Unless the Lord guards the city,
> the guard keeps watch in vain.

Psalm 139:13-18

For it was you who formed my inward parts;
> you knit me together in my mother's womb.

I praise you, for I am fearfully and wonderfully
> made.

Wonderful are your works;
that I know very well.
My frame was not hidden from you,
when I was being made in secret,
intricately woven in the depths of the earth.
Your eyes beheld my unformed substance.
In your book were written
all the days that were formed for me,
when none of them as yet existed.
How weighty to me are your thoughts, O God!
How vast is the sum of them!
I try to count them—they are more than the sand;
I come to the end—I am still with you.

Proverbs 14:26
In the fear of the Lord one has strong confidence,
and one's children will have a refuge.

Proverbs 27:11
Be wise, my child, and make my heart glad,
so that I may answer whoever reproaches me.

Ecclesiastes 4:9-12
Two are better than one, because they have a good reward for their toil. For if they fall, one will lift up the other; but woe to one who is alone and falls and does not have another to help. Again, if two lie together, they keep warm; but how can one keep warm alone? And though one might

prevail against another, two will withstand one. A threefold cord is not quickly broken.

Song of Solomon 8:7
Many waters cannot quench love,
    neither can floods drown it.
If one offered for love
    all the wealth of one's house,
    it would be utterly scorned.

Isaiah 40:28-31
Have you not known? Have you not heard?
The Lord is the everlasting God,
    the Creator of the ends of the earth.
He does not faint or grow weary;
    his understanding is unsearchable.
He gives power to the faint,
    and strengthens the powerless.
Even youths will faint and be weary,
    and the young will fall exhausted;
but those who wait for the Lord shall renew their
        strength,
    they shall mount up with wings like eagles,
they shall run and not be weary,
    they shall walk and not faint.

Isaiah 54:10
For the mountains may depart
    and the hills be removed,

but my steadfast love shall not depart from you,
> and my covenant of peace shall not be re
> moved,
> says the Lord, who has compassion on you.

Isaiah 55:6-7
Seek the Lord while he may be found,
> call upon him while he is near;
let the wicked forsake their way,
> and the unrighteous their thoughts;
let them return to the Lord, that he may have
> mercy on them,
> and to our God, for he will abundantly
> pardon.

Isaiah 61:1-3
The spirit of the Lord God is upon me,
> because the Lord has anointed me;
he has sent me to bring good news to the
> oppressed,
> to bind up the brokenhearted,
to proclaim liberty to the captives,
> and release to the prisoners;
to proclaim the year of the Lord's favor,
> and the day of vengeance of our God;
> to comfort all who mourn;
to provide for those who mourn in Zion—
> to give them a garland instead of ashes,
the oil of gladness instead of mourning,
> the mantle of praise instead of a faint spirit.

They will be called oaks of righteousness,
> the planting of the LORD, to display his glory.

Jeremiah 29:11
For surely I know the plans I have for you, says the LORD, plans for your welfare and not for harm, to give you a future with hope.

Ezekiel 37:27
My dwelling place shall be with them; and I will be their God, and they shall be my people.

Matthew 5:1-12
When Jesus saw the crowds, he went up the mountain; and after he sat down, his disciples came to him. Then he began to speak, and taught them, saying:

"Blessed are the poor in spirit, for theirs is the kingdom of heaven.

"Blessed are those who mourn, for they will be comforted.

"Blessed are the meek, for they will inherit the earth.

"Blessed are those who hunger and thirst for righteousness, for they will be filled.

"Blessed are the merciful, for they will receive mercy.

"Blessed are the pure in heart, for they will see God.

"Blessed are the peacemakers, for they will be called children of God.

"Blessed are those who are persecuted for righteousness sake, for theirs is the kingdom of heaven.

"Blessed are you when people revile you and persecute you and utter all kinds of evil against you falsely on my account. Rejoice and be glad, for your reward is great in heaven, for in the same way they persecuted the prophets who were before you."

Matthew 7:7-8
"Ask, and it will be given you; search, and you will find; knock, and the door will be opened for you. For everyone who asks receives, and everyone who searches finds, and for everyone who knocks, the door will be opened."

Matthew 11:28-30
"Come to me, all you that are weary and are carrying heavy burdens, and I will give you rest. Take my yoke upon you, and learn from me; for I am gentle and humble in heart, and you will find rest for your souls. For my yoke is easy, and my burden is light."

Matthew 25:35-40
"'[For] I was hungry and you gave me food, I was thirsty and you gave me something to drink, I was a stranger and you welcomed me, I was naked and you gave me clothing, I was sick and you took care of me, I was in prison and you visited

me.' Then the righteous will answer him, 'Lord, when was it that we saw you hungry and gave you food, or thirsty and gave you something to drink? And when was it that we saw you a stranger and welcomed you, or naked and gave you clothing? And when was it that we saw you sick or in prison and visited you?' And the king will answer them, 'Truly I tell you, just as you did it to one of the least of these who are members of my family, you did it to me.'"

Luke 6:27-31
"But I say to you that listen, Love your enemies, do good to those who hate you, bless those who curse you, pray for those who abuse you. If anyone strikes you on the cheek, offer the other also; and from anyone who takes away your coat do not withhold even your shirt. Give to everyone who begs from you; and if anyone takes away your goods, do not ask for them again. Do to others as you would have them do to you."

Luke 10:30-35
Jesus replied, "A man was going down from Jerusalem to Jericho, and fell into the hands of robbers, who stripped him, beat him, and went away, leaving him half dead. Now by chance a priest was going down that road; and when he saw him, he passed by on the other side. So likewise a Levite, when he came to the place and saw him, passed by on the other side. But a Samaritan

while traveling came near him; and when he saw him, he was moved with pity. He went to him and bandaged his wounds, having poured oil and wine on them. Then he put him on his own animal, brought him to an inn, and took care of him. The next day he took out two denarii, gave them to the innkeeper, and said, 'Take care of him; and when I come back, I will repay you whatever more you spend.'"

John 3:16-17, *King James Version*
"For God so loved the world, that he gave his only begotten Son, that whosoever believeth in him should not perish, but have everlasting life. For God sent not his Son into the world to condemn the world; but that the world through him might be saved."

John 8:12
Again Jesus spoke to them, saying "I am the light of the world. Whoever follows me will never walk in darkness but will have the light of life."

John 12:1-11
Six days before the Passover Jesus came to Bethany, the home of Lazarus, whom he had raised from the dead. There they gave a dinner for him. Martha served, and Lazarus was one of those at the table with him. Mary took a pound of costly perfume made of pure nard, anointed Jesus' feet, and wiped them with her hair. The house

was filled with the fragrance of the perfume. But Judas Iscariot, one of his disciples (the one who was about to betray him), said, "Why was this perfume not sold for three hundred denarii and the money given to the poor?" (He said this not because he cared about the poor, but because he was a thief; he kept the common purse and used to steal what was put into it.) Jesus said, "Leave her alone. She bought it so that she might keep it for the day of my burial. You always have the poor with you, but you do not always have me."

When the great crowd of the Jews learned that he was there, they came not only because of Jesus but also to see Lazarus, whom he had raised from the dead. So the chief priests planned to put Lazarus to death as well, since it was on account of him that many of the Jews were deserting and were believing in Jesus.

John 13:34-35
"I give you a new commandment, that you love one another. Just as I have loved you, you also should love one another. By this everyone will know that you are my disciples, if you have love for one another."

John 14:1-6
"Do not let your hearts be troubled. Believe in God, believe also in me. In my Father's house there are many dwelling places. If it were not so, would I have told you that I go to prepare a place

for you? And if I go and prepare a place for you, I will come again and will take you to myself, so that where I am, there you may be also. And you know the way to the place where I am going." Thomas said to him, "Lord, we do not know where you are going. How can we know the way?" Jesus said to him, "I am the way, and the truth, and the life. No one comes to the Father except through me."

John 14:23
Jesus answered him, "Those who love me will keep my word, and my Father will love them, and we will come to them and make our home with them."

John 15:9-17
"As the Father has loved me, so I have loved you; abide in my love. If you keep my commandments, you will abide in my love, just as I have kept my Father's commandments and abide in his love. I have said these things to you so that my joy may be in you, and that your joy may be complete.

"This is my commandment, that you love one another as I have loved you. No one has greater love than this, to lay down one's life for one's friends. You are my friends if you do what I command you. I do not call you servants any longer, because the servant does not know what the master is doing; but I have called you friends, because I have made known to you everything that I have heard from my Father. You did not choose me but I chose you. And I appointed you to go and bear fruit, fruit that will last, so that the Father will give you whatever you ask him in my name. I am giving you these commands so that you may love one another."

Acts 27:35
After [Paul] had said this, he took bread; and giving thanks to God in the presence of all, he broke it and began to eat.

Romans 5:1-5
Therefore, since we are justified by faith, we have peace with God through our Lord Jesus Christ, through whom we have obtained access to this grace in which we stand; and we boast in our hope of sharing the glory of God. And not only that, but we also boast in our sufferings, knowing that suffering produces endurance, and endurance produces character, and character produces hope, and hope does not disappoint us, because God's love has been poured into our hearts through the Holy Spirit that has been given to us.

Romans 8:31, 35, 37-39
What then are we to say about these things? If God is for us, who is against us? . . . Who will separate us from the love of Christ? Will hardship, or distress, or persecution, or famine, or nakedness,

or peril, or sword? . . . No, in all these things we are more than conquerors through him who loved us. For I am convinced that neither death, nor life, nor angels, nor rulers, nor things present, nor things to come, nor powers, nor height, nor depth, nor anything else in all creation, will be able to separate us from the love of God in Christ Jesus our Lord.

Romans 14:7-9
We do not live to ourselves, and we do not die to ourselves. If we live, we live to the Lord, and if we die, we die to the Lord; so then, whether we live or whether we die, we are the Lord's. For to this end Christ died and lived again, so that he might be Lord of both the dead and the living.

1 Corinthians 1:4
I give thanks to my God always for you because of the grace of God that has been given you in Christ Jesus.

1 Corinthians 13
If I speak in the tongues of mortals and of angels, but do not have love, I am a noisy gong or a clanging cymbal. And if I have prophetic powers, and understand all mysteries and all knowledge, and if I have all faith, so as to remove mountains, but do not have love, I am nothing. If I give away all my possessions, and if I hand over my body so

that I may boast, but do not have love, I gain nothing.

Love is patient; love is kind; love is not envious or boastful or arrogant or rude. It does not insist on its own way; it is not irritable or resentful; it does not rejoice in wrongdoing, but rejoices in the truth. It bears all things, believes all things, hopes all things, endures all things.

Love never ends. But as for prophecies, they will come to an end; as for tongues, they will cease; as for knowledge, it will come to an end. For we know only in part, and we prophesy only in part; but when the complete comes, the partial will come to an end. When I was a child, I spoke like a child, I thought like a child, I reasoned like a child; when I became an adult, I put an end to childish ways. For now we see in a mirror, dimly, but then we will see face to face. Now I know only in part; then I will know fully, even as I have been fully known. And now faith, hope, and love abide, these three; and the greatest of these is love.

1 Corinthians 15:50-55

What I am saying, brothers and sisters, is this: flesh and blood cannot inherit the kingdom of God, nor does the perishable inherit the imperishable. Listen, I will tell you a mystery! We will not all die, but we will all be changed, in a moment, in the twinkling of an eye, at the last trumpet. For the trumpet will sound, and the dead will be

raised imperishable, and we will be changed. For this perishable body must put on imperishability, and this mortal body must put on immortality. When this perishable body puts on imperishability, and this mortal body puts on immortality, then the saying that is written will be fulfilled:
"Death has been swallowed up in victory."
"Where, O death, is your victory?
Where, O death, is your sting?"

2 Corinthians 1:3-5
Blessed be the God and Father of our Lord Jesus Christ, the Father of mercies and the God of all consolation, who consoles us in all our affliction, so that we may be able to console those who are in any affliction with the consolation with which we ourselves are consoled by God. For just as the sufferings of Christ are abundant for us, so also our consolation is abundant through Christ.

2 Corinthians 4:5-12
For we do not proclaim ourselves; we proclaim Jesus Christ as Lord and ourselves as your slaves for Jesus' sake. For it is the God who said, "Let light shine out of darkness," who has shone in our hearts to give the light of the knowledge of the glory of God in the face of Jesus Christ.

But we have this treasure in clay jars, so that it may be made clear that this extraordinary power belongs to God and does not come from us. We are afflicted in every way, but not crushed; perplexed, but not driven to despair; persecuted, but not forsaken; struck down, but not destroyed; always carrying in the body the death of Jesus, so that the life of Jesus may also be made visible in our bodies. For while we live, we are always being given up to death for Jesus' sake, so that the life of Jesus may be made visible in our mortal flesh. So death is at work in us, but life in you.

2 Corinthians 5:17-19
So if anyone is in Christ, there is a new creation: everything old has passed away; see, everything has become new! All this is from God, who reconciled us to himself through Christ, and has given us the ministry of reconciliation; that is, in Christ God was reconciling the world to himself, not counting their trespasses against them, and entrusting the message of reconciliation to us.

2 Corinthians 9:6-15
The point is this: the one who sows sparingly will also reap sparingly, and the one who sows bountifully will also reap bountifully. Each of you must give as you have made up your mind, not reluctantly or under compulsion, for God loves a cheerful giver. And God is able to provide you with every blessing in abundance, so that by always having enough of everything, you may share abundantly in every good work. As it is written,

> "He scatters abroad, he gives to the poor;
> his righteousness endures forever."

He who supplies seed to the sower and bread for food will supply and multiply your seed for sowing and increase the harvest of your righteousness. You will be enriched in every way for your great generosity, which will produce thanksgiving to God through us; for the rendering of this ministry not only supplies the needs of the saints but also overflows with many thanksgivings to God. Through the testing of this ministry you glorify God by your obedience to the confession of the gospel of Christ and by the generosity of your sharing with them and with all others, while they long for you and pray for you because of the surpassing grace of God that he has given you. Thanks be to God for his indescribable gift!

Galatians 6:2
Bear one another's burdens, and in this way you will fulfill the law of Christ.

Ephesians 2:10
For we are what he has made us, created in Christ Jesus for good works, which God prepared beforehand to be our way of life.

Ephesians 4:31-32
Put away from you all bitterness and wrath and anger and wrangling and slander, together with all malice, and be kind to one another, tender-

hearted, forgiving one another, as God in Christ has forgiven you.

Philippians 1:3-6
I thank my God every time I remember you, constantly praying with joy in every one of my prayers for all of you, because of your sharing in the gospel from the first day until now. I am confident of this, that the one who began a good work among you will bring it to completion by the day of Jesus Christ.

Philippians 2:1-4
If then there is any encouragement in Christ, any consolation from love, any sharing in the Spirit, any compassion and sympathy, make my joy complete: be of the same mind, having the same love, being in full accord and of one mind. Do nothing from selfish ambition or conceit, but in humility regard others as better than yourselves. Let each of you look not to your own interests, but to the interests of others.

Philippians 4:6
Do not worry about anything, but in everything by prayer and supplication with thanksgiving let your requests be made known to God.

1 Thessalonians 5:16-18
Rejoice always, pray without ceasing, give thanks in all circumstances; for this is the will of God in Christ Jesus for you.

1 Timothy 4:4-5
For everything created by God is good, and nothing is to be rejected, provided it is received with thanksgiving; for it is sanctified by God's word and by prayer.

Hebrews 6:10
For God is not unjust; he will not overlook your work and the love that you showed for his sake in serving the saints, as you still do.

James 5:13-15, *Contemporary English Version*
If you are having trouble you should pray. And if you are feeling good you should sing praises. If you are sick ask the church leaders to come and pray for you. Ask them to put olive oil on you in the name of the Lord. If you have faith when you pray for sick people, they will get well. The Lord will heal them, and if they have sinned, he will forgive them.

James 5:16
Therefore confess your sins to one another, and pray for one another, so that you may be healed. The prayer of the righteous is powerful and effective.

1 Peter 5:6-7
Humble yourselves therefore under the mighty hand of God, so that he may exalt you in due time. Cast all your anxiety on him, because he cares for you.

1 John 4:7-12
Beloved, let us love one another, because love is from God; everyone who loves is born of God and knows God. Whoever does not love does not know God, for God is love. God's love was revealed among us in this way: God sent his only Son into the world so that we might live through him. In this is love, not that we loved God but that he loved us and sent his Son to be the atoning sacrifice for our sins. Beloved, since God loved us so much, we also ought to love one another. No one has ever seen God; if we love one another, God lives in us, and his love is perfected in us.

3 John 2
Beloved, I pray that all may go well with you and that you may be in good health, just as it is well with your soul.

Revelation 21:1-4; 22:5, *King James Version*
And I saw a new heaven and a new earth: for the first heaven and the first earth were passed away; and there was no more sea. And I, John, saw the holy city, new Jerusalem, coming down from God out of heaven, prepared as a bride adorned for her husband. And I heard a great voice out of heaven, saying,
> "Behold the tabernacle of God is with men
>   and he will dwell with them,
>   and they shall be his people,

>   and God himself shall be with them,
>   and be their God.
> And God shall wipe away all tears from their eyes;
>   and there shall be no more death,
>   neither sorrow, nor crying,
>   neither shall there be any more pain:
>   for the former things are passed away."

"And there shall be no night there; and they need no candle, neither light of the sun; for the Lord God giveth them light: and they shall reign forever and ever."

INDEX

A

abuse
    hymns, 25-26
    prayers, 22-25
    scriptures, 25
    See also Volume I, pp. 8, 9, 50, 59

accident (prayer), 31-32

addiction
    hymns, 19-20
    prayers, 14-19
    scriptures, 19
    See also Volume I, pp. 9, 11

adoption (prayer), 93-94

aged. *See* older adults

anniversary
    hymns, 90
    prayers, 89-90
    scriptures, 90

Annual Conference statements
    1998 statement, 7
    See also Volume I, pp. 5-6, 103-4, 106-7, 121-22,
        128, 172, 173

anointing
    at home, 107
    biblical basis for, 100, 102-103, 104
    Brethren understanding of, 100-104
    children and, 108-9, 114-17
    death and, 109, 122-23
    definition, 102-3
    divorced persons, 120-21

180 Deacon Manual—Caring

    expectations of, 102, 103, 107
    grandparents for raising grandchildren, 123-26
    healing and, 100-104, 108
    history of, 102-3
    hymns, 11-12, 112, 126
    interest in, 106-7
    invitation to, 105-7
    Jesus and healing, 103, 104
    laying on of hands, 104, 105, 114, 117
    listening during, 108
    logistics, 105-7
    new members and, 99, 105
    oil, 100, 102, 103, 104, 106, 111, 110-17
    prayers, 117-26
    preparation for, 107-8
    reconciliation and, 102, 108, 120
    role of deacons in, 12, 99, 100
    scriptures used during, 100, 108, 110, 111-12, 115
    services, 109-17
    special situations and, 108-9, 119-26
    surgery and, 33-34, 121-22
    symbolism of, 102, 104
    testimonies of, 106
    touching and, 104, 105, 111, 113-14
    unconscious persons and, 109
    words spoken during, 110-11
    worship resources, 109-26
    worship service, as part of regular, 105-6
    See also Volume I, pp. 20, 21-23, 57, 80-81, 173-75

B

baptism
    adult baptism, 148
    believers baptism, 148-49
    candidates seeking, 134

    definition, 148-49
    feetwashing as symbol of cleansing, 138
    Jesus' example, 148
    love feast as expression of renewal of, 135
    preparation for, 149
    role of deacons in, 12, 99, 149
    symbolism of, 149
    trine immersion, 149
    See also Volume I, pp. 16, 37, 105, 173-74

Bible
    anointing and the, 100, 102-103, 104
    full text of scriptures, 151-78
    interpretation of, 9
    language and, 8-11
    Lord's Prayer, 4-5
    love feast and the, 128-30
    reading out loud, 8-11
    resource for deacon ministry, 8
    rule of faith and practice, 7
    translations, 8, 10
    See also scriptures

birth
    hymns, 94
    prayers, 92-94
    scriptures, 94

birthday
    hymns, 87
    prayers, 85-87
    scriptures, 87

blessings, house
    hymns, 72
    prayers, 67-71
    scriptures, 72

blessings, meal
    hymns, 96-97

prayers, 96
scriptures, 96
bread and cup communion, 130, 141, 146

C

caregivers
    deacons as, v, 13 (*see also* Volume I, pp. 5, 58, 69-75, 103, 119-20, 456-57)
    hymns, 84
    prayers, 81-83
    scriptures, 83-84
    See also Volume I, pp. 20, 97-98, 99-101
celebrations
    anniversary, 89-90
    birthday, 85-87
    birth or adoption, 92-94
    meal blessings, 96-97
children and youth
    adoption (prayer), 93-94
    anointing and, 108-9, 114-17
    birth (prayer), 92-94
    birthday (prayer), 85-87
    blessing of during house blessing, 71
    divorce and (prayer), 77-78
    domestic abuse and (prayer), 22
    graduation (prayer), 50
    grandparents caring for (prayer), 83, 123-26
    illness and (prayer), 32-33
    leaving home (prayer), 47-50
    love feast and, 133, 134, 145-46
    miscarriage or stillbirth (prayer), 57-58, 63-64
    scriptures and, 50-51
    See also Volume I, pp. 8, 19, 20-21, 66-69, 100, 175
chronic illness (prayer), 54
communion
    bread and cup, 130, 141, 146

    bread, making of, 131, 136
    children and, 145-46
    feetwashing, 129, 130, 132, 133, 136, 137-39
    history of, 129-31
    hymns, 145
    love feast (*see* love feast)
    Maundy Thursday, 130
    older adults and (*see* Volume I, p. 57)
    preparation for, 129-33
    role of deacons in, 128-36
    World Communion Sunday, 130
    See also love feast
    See also Volume I, pp. 16, 34-35, 57, 115-16, 173-74, 185

conflict (prayer), 41-44. *See also* reconciliation

congregations
    anointing and, 105-7, 108
    baptism and, 148-49
    Bible translations and, 10
    conflict (prayer), 43
    love feast and, 130, 131-32, 133-35, 145-46
    support of by deacons, 13, 85 (*see also* Volume I)

crises
    abuse (*see* abuse)
    addiction (*see* addiction)
    anointing during, 105, 107
    children and (*see* Volume I, pp. 68-69)
    conflict (*see* reconciliation)
    death (*see* death)
    definition, 13
    divorce (*see* divorce)
    domestic violence (*see* abuse)
    illness and injury (*see* illness)
    natural disaster (*see* natural disaster)
    praying during, 5-6, 7

184 *Deacon Manual—Caring*

    surgery (*see* surgery)
    unemployment (*see* unemployment)
    See also Volume I, pp. 83-85, 173-75

D

deacons
    anointing and, 100-109 (*see also* Volume I, pp. 21-23, 57, 80-81)
    hymns in ministry, 11-12
    love feast and, 128-36
    ordinances and, 12, 99
    prayer in ministry, 2-7
    scripture in ministry, 7-11
death
    anointing and, 109, 122-23
    bedside prayers, 54-56
    child or infant (prayer), 56-57
    chronic illness (prayer), 54
    dying person (prayer), 53
    hymns, 60
    miscarriage or stillbirth (prayer), 57-58, 63-64
    older adult (prayer), 54
    prayers, 53-59
    Psalm 23, 153-54
    scriptures, 59-60
    suicide (prayer), 58-59
    unexpected (prayer), 53
disabled persons
    handwashing, 136
    love feast and, 132
divorce
    anointing and, 120-21
    children and youth and (prayer), 77-78
    hymns, 79
    prayers, 74-78

scriptures, 79
See also Volume I, pp. 10, 83, 85
domestic violence. *See* abuse.

E

elderly. *See* older adults
emergencies
    See crises
    See also Volume I, pp. 7, 51, 61, 68-69, 100
emotional healing, 13, 101, 105, 106, 117
employment, loss of. *See* unemployment
end of life. *See* death

F

feetwashing
    alternatives to, 132, 136
    discomfort with, 133
    handwashing as alternative, 132, 136
    hymns, 145
    love feast and, 129, 130
    meditation, 137-39
    new members and, 133
    older adults and, 136
    preparation for, 132
    scriptures used during, 137
    worship resources, 137-39, 145
    See also Volume I, p. 4
financial stability (prayer), 64
flood, aftermath of (prayer), 38

G

graduation (prayer), 50
grandparents
    anointing for raising grandchildren, 123-26
    birth of grandchild (prayer), 92-94
    caring for grandchildren (prayer), 83

grief and loss
    hymns, 65
    prayers, 62-64
    scriptures, 65
    See also death
    See also loss
    See also Volume I, pp. 69-75

H

handwashing, 132, 136
healing
    abuse (*see* abuse)
    addiction (*see* addiction)
    anointing and, 100-104, 108
    Brethren understanding of, 100-102
    conflict (*see* reconciliation)
    divorce (*see* divorce)
    hymns, 126
    illness (*see* illness)
    Jesus and, 104
    loss (*see* loss)
    prayers, 117-19
    scriptures, 110, 176
    surgery (*see* surgery)
    testimonies of, 106
    thanksgiving for healing (prayer), 33
home
    anointing in the, 107
    blessing, 70-72 (*see also* house blessings)
    children leaving (prayer), 47-50
    housewarming (prayer), 69
    meal blessings (*see* meal blessings)
    moving to a new (prayer), 67-69
    older adults leaving (prayer), 68-69
    visitation, 1, 11 (*see also* Volume I, pp. 38-40, 58-61)

Index 187

honesty in prayer, 5-6
hospital
    anointing in the, 107
    surgery (prayer), 33-34 (*see also* surgery)
    visitation, 1, 11 (*see also* Volume I, pp. 75-83)
    See also illness
house blessings
    hymns, 72
    prayers, 67-69
    scriptures, 72
    service, 70-72
hurricane/tornado, aftermath of (prayer), 38. *See also* natural disaster
hymns
    abuse, 25-26
    addiction, 19-20
    adoption, 94
    anniversary, 90
    anointing, 11-12, 112, 126
    birth, 94
    birthday, 87
    caregiving, 84
    children leaving home, 51
    closing of worship, 145
    communion, 145
    conflict, 45
    divorce, 79
    domestic violence, 25-26
    end of life, 60
    feetwashing, 145
    house blessing, 72
    illness, 35
    loss, 65
    love feast, 145
    meal blessing, 96-97

188   Deacon Manual—Caring

    ministry with, 11-12
    natural disaster, 39
    new child, 94
    opening of worship, 145
    reconciliation, 45
    relocation, 72
    surgery, 35

I

illness
    accident (prayer), 31-32
    anointing, 107-8 (*see also* anointing)
    caregiving and (*see* Volume I, pp. 99-101)
    children and (prayer), 32-33
    chronic (prayer), 54
    hymns, 35
    laying on of hands, 104
    mental (*see* Volume I, pp. 9, 91-94)
    prayers, 28-34, 117-19
    scriptures, 35
    self-image and (*see* Volume I, pp. 78-80)
    surgery (*see* surgery)
    thanksgiving for healing (prayer), 33
    See also Volume I, pp. 21-23, 48, 70, 75-80, 91-94,
injury. *See* illness

L

laying on of hands, 104, 105, 114, 117
life transitions
    caregiving (*see* caregivers)
    children leaving home (*see* children and youth)
    definition, 47
    divorce (*see* divorce)
    end of life (*see* death)
    illness (*see* illness)

Index   189

    loss (*see* loss)
    relocation (*see* home)
Lord's Prayer (framework for prayer), 4-5
Lord's Supper. *See* love feast *and* communion
loss
    divorce (*see* divorce)
    employment, 64
    financial stability (prayer), 64
    hymns, 65
    miscarriage or stillbirth (prayer), 57-58, 63-64
    prayers, 62-64
    quality of life (prayer), 63
    relationship (prayer), 62-63 (*see also* divorce)
    scriptures, 65
    security, 13
    See also death
    See also Volume I, pp. 69-75
love feast
    alternatives, 131-32, 135-36
    annual visit (*see* Volume I, pp. 34-35)
    attendance, encouraging, 131, 133-35
    bread and cup communion, 130, 146
    changes in format, 131-32, 135-36
    children and, 133, 134, 145-46
    communion (*see* communion)
    feetwashing, 129, 130, 132, 133, 136
    history of, 129-31
    hymns, 11, 145
    menu planning for, 131, 136
    new members and, 132-33, 134-35
    participation in, 129, 131-36, 145-46
    prayers, 140-41
    preparation for, 131-33
    role of deacons in, 128-36
    scriptures used during, 128, 130, 137

worship resources, 137-45
See also Volume I, pp. 1, 4, 14, 16, 57, 115-16, 173-74

M

meal blessings
    hymns, 96-97
    prayers, 96
    scriptures, 96
members, new. *See* new members
mental health ministry
    addiction (*see* addiction)
    deacons and (*see* Volume I, pp. 19, 91-94)
    medical professionals, 101
menu (love feast)
    alternatives, 131, 135-36
    communion bread, 131
    planning, 131
milestones
    anniversary, 89-90
    birth or adoption, 92-94
    birthday, 85-87
moving to a new home (*see* home)
music and hymns
    See hymns
    See also Volume I, pp. 9, 14, 40, 64, 76-77, 161, 164

N

natural disaster
    hymns, 39
    prayers, 37-38
    scriptures, 39
    See also Volume I, pp. 83, 84-85
new child
    hymns, 94

prayers, 92-94
scriptures, 94
new members
    anointing and, 99, 105
    love feast and, 132-33, 134-35
    ordinances and, 133
nursing facilities, 1. *See also* Volume I, pp. 61-63

O

oil, anointing, 100, 102, 103, 104, 106, 111, 110-17
older adults
    anointing and (*see* Volume I, pp. 21-23, 57, 80-81)
    change of residence (prayer), 68-69
    death (prayer), 54
    feetwashing and, 136
    grandparents, 83, 92-94, 123-26
    loss of quality of life (prayer), 63
    memory loss (*see* Volume I, pp. 94-98)
    ordinances, adaptations for, 136
    visitation (*see* Volume I, pp. 56, 58-65, 75-77)
    See also Volume I, pp. 7, 20, 54-66, 94-98
ordinances
    anointing (*see* anointing)
    baptism (*see* baptism)
    communion (*see* communion)
    feetwashing (*see* feetwashing)
    love feast (*see* love feast)
    new members and, 99, 105, 132-33, 134-35
    See also Volume I

P

parents
    birth or adoption (prayer), 92-94
    children leaving home (prayer), 47-50
    child with illness (anointing), 114-17

    child with illness (prayer), 32-33
    divorce (prayer), 74-78
    graduation of child (prayer), 50
    grandparents (*see* grandparents)
    love feast (education), 134
    pregnancy (prayer), 92
prayers
    abuse, 22-25
    addiction, 14-19
    anniversary, 89-90
    anointing, 117-26
    basic framework, 4-6
    birth, 92-94
    birthday, 85-87
    caregiving, 81-83
    children leaving home, 47-50
    conflict, 41-44
    death, 53-59
    divorce, 74-78
    domestic violence, 22-25
    during visitation, 2-7 (*see also* Volume I, pp. 19, 40, 41, 46-49, 64, 80, 82-83, 99)
    end of life, 53-59
    healing, 33, 117-19
    helps for leading, 6-7
    honesty in, 5-6
    house blessing, 67-71
    illness, 28-34, 117-19
    Lord's Prayer, 4-5
    loss, 62-64 (*see also* death)
    love feast, 140-41
    meal blessing, 96
    ministry with, 2-7
    miscarriage or stillbirth, 57-58, 63-64
    natural disaster, 37-38

new child, 92-94
   power of, 2-7
   praying the Psalms, 6 (*see also* Volume I, p. 141)
   pregnancy, 92
   reconciliation, 41-44
   suicide, 58-59
   surgery, 33-34
   See also Volume I
pregnancy (prayer), 92
priesthood of all believers, 3-4
prison ministry. *See* Volume I, pp. 85-91
Psalms, praying the, 6
purpose of *Deacon Manual*, vi-viii

R

reading scripture, 8-11
reconciliation
   anointing and, 102, 108, 120
   hymns, 45
   prayers, 41-44
   scriptures, 45
   See also Volume I, pp. 23-32, 43, 128, 163, 173-75
relocation (*see* home)

S

scriptures
   abuse, 25
   addiction, 19
   anniversary, 90
   anointing, 100, 108, 110, 111-12, 115
   birth, 94
   birthday, 87
   burdens, 164, 174
   caregiving, 83-84
   children leaving home, 50-51

comfort and consolation, 153-54, 162-63, 163-64,
    172, 175
conflict, 45
cry for help, 153, 155, 156
death, 59-60
divorce, 79
domestic violence, 25
end of life, 59-60
feetwashing, 137
full text of, 151-78
healing, 110, 176
help from God, 153, 155-56, 159
house blessing, 72
illness, 35
John 3:16, 166
loss, 65
love feast, 128, 130, 137
love of God, 154-55, 157, 161-62, 166, 167, 168-70,
    177
loving others, 167, 168-69, 177
Matthew 18 (*see* Volume I, pp. 24, 27-29, 128, 159)
meal blessing, 96
ministry with, 7-11
natural disaster, 39
new child, 94
peace, 151, 161-62, 163-64, 169
prayer, 2, 153, 156, 165, 175-77
praying the Psalms, 6 (*see also* Volume I, p. 141)
presence of God, 152, 153, 155-56, 163, 167-68,
    169-70, 177-78
private reading of (*see* Volume I, pp. 139-41)
Psalm 23, 153-54
reconciliation, 45 (*see also* Volume I, pp. 27-29)
sorrow, 153, 177-78
strength from God, 155-56, 161

suicide, 59
surgery, 35
translations, 8, 10
See also Volume I, pp. 2-5, 36, 103, 133, 153-54
seniors. *See* older adults
separation. *See* divorce
services (worship)
- anointing, basic, 110-11
- anointing, child, 114-17
- anointing, detailed, 111-14
- anointing, grandparents for raising grandchildren, 123-26
- fellowship meal liturgy, 141-43
- house blessing, 70-72
- *See also* love feast

suicide (prayer), 58-59
surgery
- anointing and, 121-22
- hymns, 35
- prayers, 33-34
- scriptures, 35
- *See also* Volume I, pp. 22, 75-77, 80-83

T

tests, hospital (prayer), 34
tornado/hurricane, aftermath of (prayer), 38. *See also* natural disaster
touching, 104, 105, 111, 113-14. *See also* Volume I, pp. 42, 49, 64
transitions (*see* life transitions)
translations (Bible), 8, 10

U

unconscious, ministry to the, 109. *See also* Volume I, pp. 98-99 unemployment, 62, 64. *See also* Volume I, pp. 10, 11, 68, 71, 83, 85

unity, 41-45, 108, 120. *See also* Volume I, pp. 23-32

V

victim of abuse (prayer), 22-24

visitation, guidelines for. *See* Volume I

W

worship resources
>*See* anointing
>*See* feetwashing
>*See* love feast
>*See also* Volume I

Y

youth. *See* children and youth

ISBN 978-0-87178-181-9